# How to Raise an Entrepreneur:

## 15 Business Plans for Kids & Teens
## To Make Money on a Saturday

*By David T. Fagan*

*1. Understanding Your Child's Personality*
*2. What Motivates Your Child?*
*3. Secrets of Success*

How to Raise an Entrepreneur: 15 Business Plans for Kids & Teens to Make Money on a Saturday

Published by On The Inside Press

Printed in the United States of America.

ISBN 978-0-9829153-3-2

**Contact David Fagan at dfaganbusiness@gmail.com.**

## Dedication

To Mom and Dad (Vern and Lenora Fagan) who always made me believe I could do anything. They built the heart and mind of my Entrepreneurial Soul. I only hope I can give my kids the same self-confidence to follow their dreams.

DTF

## Acknowledgements

To Aaron Halderman and his daughter Abree, a huge thank you.

I also want to thank Candace Morehouse who helped me write this in the middle of so many other projects.

DTF

# Contents

## Introduction

*"When you're a self-made man you start very early in life. In my case it was at nine years old when I started bringing income into the family. You get a drive that's a little different, maybe a little stronger, than somebody who inherited."* – Kirk Kerkorian, CEO Tracinda Corporation

How young is too young to become an entrepreneur? Is nine years old too early for a child to make his or her own money? When it comes to teaching your children business skills, is it ever too early? Before you answer these questions, let's consider the reasons children should learn to become young entrepreneurs.

If you are like many parents, the recessionary economy has taught you a hard lesson: everything you've earned over the years, every career move up the corporate ladder, every asset that you've acquired, all of your retirement savings – all of it can be gone in a flash. There is no such thing as a "secure" job. Everyone can be affected by an economic downturn, no matter if you are a CEO or a laborer.

In light of recent economic factors, many of us made a decision to step out of our role as employee and start our own business. When one door closed, we created a new door to open, full of possibilities and reliant only on our own fortitude and determination for success. If this describes you, great! If not, you were one of the lucky ones who didn't have to worry about creating a new source of income.

What about your kids? What do you want for them? Should they learn lessons about business now or wait until it's absolutely necessary, later in life?

Many parents keep the details of family hardships from their kids, trying to make them believe that everything is status quo when, in fact, they can't figure out how to pay the monthly household bills. It might surprise you to know that most kids want to be involved in the family's affairs, good or bad. Besides, trying to protect them from stress and problems really isn't beneficial.

Instead, consider turning your hardship into a teachable moment. Show them the value of good financial and business decision-making now. The future will seem a lot less frightening if they are taught how to take control of it.

Unfortunately, our school systems don't include such topics as business development and financial management in the curriculum. That responsibility falls to the parents. More important now than ever, self-sufficiency, good decision-making, and the ability to manage money are vital skills for anyone growing up in this age of higher prices, economic uncertainty, and the proliferation of erroneous information provided by the World Wide Web. How are you going to teach your children the skills necessary to not only survive, but thrive, no matter the local or national and global circumstances?

Teaching by example is always good. After all, we can't expect our kids to do as we say, not as we do. But observation is only one small way to acquire knowledge. Hands-on experience has proven to be much more effective. In addition to developing good behaviors by doing, kids are motivated to continue these behaviors by receiving a reward – and what better reward than earning money to purchase something valuable to them?

We'll discuss goals later in this book, but I want you to start thinking about what is valuable to your children. Is it the latest video game system? The newest techno-gadget? A trendy outfit from the mall? The real answer might just surprise you.

The one thing that most kids want from their parents is more time together; and not just more time, but quality time doing things that are fun for everyone. Study after study over the past several decades has confirmed that kids want more of *you*. All too often parents are stressed from work and responsibility and the little time they do designate for their children is not quality time. Helping your child start his or her own business is a fantastic way to work toward a common goal, learn new skills, and bond on a deeper level.

Another benefit of raising a young entrepreneur is that it teaches them financial responsibility. In this age when kids are inundated by commercial messages conveying the latest, newest, most improved toys, gadgets, junk food, and clothing they must have it's hard to rein them in and make them understand the value of more important pursuits. They are taught at an early age to want; rarely are they taught an alternative to the mindless frenzy of materialism. Their self-worth is defined by possessions.

In a successful business, you can't just spend money without putting thought into what will make a positive difference for the future. Success is driven by dependability, motivation, good decision-making, honesty, creativity, and so much more. That is what young entrepreneurs learn.

And what about you? What's the most valuable thing you can give your kids?

Parents often have a laundry list of things they want for their children. These might include being a good person, being well behaved, being responsible, making a positive difference in the world, or caring for others. I don't know of a single parent who has ever said, "I want my son or daughter to fail, to be reliant on others, and have no work ethic."

You bought this book for a reason. Chances are you fall into one of two categories:

1) You want your kid to succeed and have lots of opportunities but really don't know where to start or how to get help

   OR

2) You are helping your kids succeed and become self-reliant and want them to receive the maximum benefit from what they have been taught.

So what is a good age to start children on the road to entrepreneurship? It varies according to the maturity level and motivation of the child, but when he or she starts taking an interest in money – where it comes from, how it is earned, why there are limits to spending power – it is a good indication that they are ready to go into business.

I have a passion for helping kids and families. As the father of seven children, I've often thought of the problems kids face, as well as the opportunities for youngsters of which many families aren't aware.

I have learned a lot from people just like you, as well as from raising my oldest daughter, Jordan. If I'd only known what I know now back when my first child was born, things would have been different in our household right from the beginning. Luckily, I am blessed that Jordan, along with my other children, has a true desire to follow in her father's footsteps and become an entrepreneur herself. I am excited to take that desire and help her to fulfill her goals in every way I possibly can.

In fact, I can't take full credit for this book, Without Jordan, the idea to help kids become entrepreneurs would never have gotten off the ground.

It all started with Jordan wanting to attend the National Speakers Association Youth Conference in New York City. That's a real worthwhile goal and I could have told her I would happily pay the expense so that she could reap the benefits of attending this conference. But after thinking about it further, I decided this was a great opportunity to teach her the value of a dollar. I told her she would have to earn the cost of transportation and lodging; a total of about $700.

Although she expressed some trepidation about her ability to earn that much money in a short amount of time, Jordan was game. She and I sat down together – enjoying some quality time – and brainstormed ideas for moneymaking activities that would allow her to earn the money in three months. I committed to helping her, but ultimately it was her own motivation that allowed her to achieve success.

And Jordan was successful. I drove her around our neighborhood and she went door-to-door offering to wash cars. Her grandma helped her plan a chicken enchilada lunch offered for sale to employees at nearby office complexes. It didn't even take her the full three months to earn more money than she needed for the trip.

It was a win-win situation. Jordan learned responsibility, financial management, and so much more. She was rewarded by the New York trip, which she enjoyed immensely. And I felt she'd learned some extremely valuable lessons – ones that will serve her throughout the rest of her life.

So no matter what your kids want, whether it is a college education or a computer or a car, consider teaching them how to earn it. Sure it's easy to just give them what they want, but when children work for it themselves, they learn skills that are far more valuable. Remember the old adage: *Give a man a fish and he will eat for a day; teach a man to fish and he will eat for a lifetime.*

In the following chapters, we will look at personality differences and safety concerns for each age, how to find your child's motivators, planning for goals, ways to ensure success, exercises the whole family can do, and how to teach your kids business basics. In addition to this information, I also provide business plans at the end of each chapter so your child can get started right away. These teachings and business plans have stirred quite an interest, evolving into Cash Club for Kids, a membership website and program for children and parents alike. I encourage you to sign up at www.cashclubkids.com and join this fast-growing community. The information and opportunities there provide an excellent adjunct to this book, along with additional resources. You can also email me at dfaganbusiness@gmail.com if you need help or have questions.

Raising an entrepreneur is an exciting journey full of ample rewards. What are you waiting for? Let's get started now. The business plans in this book are geared to your kids, but comments for you are in the **How to Make it Safe** section. Jordan's first two moneymaking ventures are included here and are sure to get you and your child ready to begin the exciting journey to entrepreneurship.

## Business Plan for a Door-to-Door Car Wash

### General Description

This business is perfect for kids aged: 8 – 17 years old

**Mission Statement**: To provide a necessary service to people too busy or unable to perform this task themselves.

**Goals and Objectives**: The goal is to create a business that provides a good source of income by working weekends and summers. The objective is to build a reputation for great service and increase sales each month via word of mouth.

**Business Philosophy**: Provide a valuable service for a good price.

**Marketing**: This service will be marketed to neighbors, housewives and mothers, friends' parents, anyone with a dirty car, truck, or motorcycle!

Competitive strengths are in convenience to the customer and performing all the little details important to each customer.

Pricing structure is donations or set a fair price.

**What this business teaches** – Face to face communication, how to work fast to earn more money quickly, how to face rejection and go on to the next job, making a sales presentation.

### Operational Plan

**Inventory: What You'll Need**

- Large mop bucket on wheels
- 6-10 towels

- Hose sprayer attachment
- Squeegee
- Car wash sponges
- Car wash soap
- Tire cleaner
- Window cleaner
- Hose (just in case)
- Stepladder
- Cash box or money bag

**What You Do**

This is a good business to do on a warmer day because people don't want to leave their houses to get their cars washed when it's hot. Saturdays are best. More people are typically home.

Get all of your supplies together and put them in your bucket. Load it all up in the car and find a street with a lot of mature trees and cars parked in the driveway or on the street.

Start at the beginning of the street and go to each house. Your child is going to get a lot of no's and no answers. That's okay because they'll get some yes's too. It's their job to find the yes's.

Knock on the door and give the script. Be excited and show enthusiasm so people will know that this is something you want to do. Remember, this is your business.

When you get a yes, signal to your parent and hook up the spray nozzle to the person's hose or to yours if they don't have one. Make sure your bucket is filled up about half way and has enough soap bubbles.

Get the car wet and start washing with the sponge. Try to get the top of the car or have your parent help you. If you are using a stepladder, be careful that it doesn't get wet to prevent slipping and falling. Make sure that you get it clean, but this shouldn't take more than 7-10 minutes, if that.

Use the squeegee and soap to do a quick wash on the windows and tires, but don't take too long because you're going to wash them again. Then spray the car off with the hose, making sure to get all the soap off.

Dry the car off with the towels but leave the windows and tires wet. Use the window cleaner and squeegee to give the windows a good shine. Try not to get the cleaner on the car but if you do, wipe it off. Spray the tires with the tire cleaner and use the sponge to get it clean. Pick one older towel that you will use all day to wipe the tires dry. Plan on this getting ruined.

Return the hose to the proper place and wind it up. Thank the customer for allowing you to wash their car and collect the money.

Secure your money in the cash box or money bag.

Go to the next house and try it again!

## How to Make it Safe

As a parent, you don't need to go to the door with your child - and actually it is better if you don't so that your child can give the pitch by themselves – but you should be close enough that the person at the door can see you. This will help them feel more comfortable that your child isn't alone and assure them that they are going to get a good car wash.

Make sure your child knows the dangers of the chemicals they are using and make sure they don't get it in their eyes or mouth.

Also, if your child is going to be washing cars outdoors on sunny days you'll want to make sure they wear sunscreen or something to protect them from sunburns and keep them hydrated by drinking lots of water.

### Script

Hi my name is _____ and I'm doing a young entrepreneur project. I'm earning money for _____. Would you like me to wash your car?

If they ask how much it is say, "I'm taking donations so it's however much you think the job I do is worth."

*Marketing Plan*

The main methods of marketing will be word of mouth and referrals. Be sure to take your child's business cards with you and have them hand one out to each customer.

You guys may also want to create a simple flyer than you can post in your neighborhood that lists the services you provide, the days you are available to work, and your home phone number. Be careful of where you place it though, and don't let your child ever use their own cell phone number. The flyer should mention that your child will be hand washing each car, their attention to detail, and that the cleaning products used are safe for a vehicle's finish – this differentiates their business from the competition. Use color to grab people's attention; you can print a flyer on colored paper or use full color images.

Spread the word of your child's business to coworkers, local businesses, your church congregation, relatives, neighbors, and friends. Keep their business cards and flyers handy to give out.

Don't forget to market online, either. Your child can post to their Facebook and/or Twitter account that they are now the proud owner of their own business.

## Finances

It's a good idea to keep a cash box or money bag in the car to put the car wash proceeds in.

At the end of the day, have your child count up their earnings. Help them keep track of the earnings in a spreadsheet or a manual table so they know how much they've earned.

Explain that their money will earn interest if your child opens a savings account at the bank and makes regular deposits.

If you provided the money for your child's supplies, have them pay you back from the proceeds of their first car wash. This will help them learn responsibility.

***Jordan's Tip****: This is a great business for hot summer days – have fun and use the hose to keep cool!*

## Business Plan for a
## Chicken Enchilada Sale

### *General Description*

This business is perfect for kids aged: 8 – 17 years old, especially if they like to cook

**Mission Statement**: To provide a tasty and affordable meal to busy families and office employees.

**Goals and Objectives**: The goal is to create a business that provides a good source of income during the summer months. The objective is to build a reputation for great food and encourage repeat business.

**Business Philosophy**: Provide a quality time- and money-saving service.

**Marketing**: Chicken enchilada lunches will be marketed to people who work in office complexes or buildings.

Competitive strengths are in convenience to the customer and providing a home-cooked meal to replace fast food lunches.

Pricing structure is based on cost of supplies; $15 per dozen is suggested at today's prices.

**What this business teaches** - Sanitation, not buying too much product, estimating costs and profits, face to face and phone communication, making a sales presentations, and making a presentation for a loan.

### *Operational Plan*

**Inventory: What You'll Need**

Ingredients per 3 dozen Chicken Enchiladas:

- 3-14 oz cans cream of chicken soup
- 16 oz sour cream
- 2 cups grated cheese (Cheddar, Colby jack, or longhorn)
- 3 chicken breasts, cooked and shredded
- ½ to 1 onion, minced
- 1-4 oz can green chilies
- 36 corn tortillas
- Oil

**Other Supplies:**

- Gloves
- Clean plastic tablecloth (optional)
- 9" x 13" pan
- Aluminum Foil
- 10 lb block ice
- Address labels (3111 or 3113 Avery) (optional)
- Phone (to get orders)
- Ice Chest
- Car (to get ingredients and deliver orders)
- Enchilada Order Form
- Office Order Form
- The Script

**What You Do**

Set aside two days for this job. For the first time, don't take too many orders, or it will turn into an overwhelming job. A good number is 9 or 12 dozen.

**First Day**

Figure out where you are going to get your orders from. Print up the order form and hit the phones. Call people from church, your friends' parents, family friends, work friends, etc. Make sure that you are professional and let them know that this is a business. You should pick a specific goal or trip you're working toward so that they will be more likely to buy. Some goals you may want to mention are a plane ticket to a fun location; a ticket to an entrepreneurial event; going to camp; buying clothes; saving for college; donations to a charity or needy family. Make sure that you've practiced the script.

If you are planning on selling in office buildings, attach an Office Order Form to a large manila envelope for each building. Write down who ordered, how many dozen they ordered, how much they need to pay, and if they're interested in ordering next time. Have one person be responsible for collecting for the office so that when you drop off the enchiladas, you can count the money and leave.

Try to get orders by the threes so that you don't have leftover materials that eat into your profits. Once you have your orders, go and buy your materials. Make sure that you have a sanitized area to work from. You may consider covering the table with a clean plastic disposable tablecloth. When handling food, wear disposable gloves and keep long hair braided and all hair out of your face. You'll be tempted, but don't lick anything. Make sure that when you're not using the ingredients, they are kept refrigerated. Wash your hands and utensils often.

Cook the chicken, keeping it separated by batch so that you will have the right amount. Boil the chicken until it is tender. This should take about an hour per batch, but you can cook several batches at once. Cook on high until it starts to boil and then turn down gradually to a medium low temperature. It should stay simmering the whole time. After it is cooked, take it out of the water and let it cool until it is warm. Shred the chicken and store it in a sealed container in the fridge until tomorrow.

### Second Day

Prepare your clean work area, put your hair back and put your gloves on your clean hands. In a large bowl, mix all ingredients for one batch except for the tortillas. Separate the mixture into three equal sized bowls. In each bowl, draw two lines to separate it into quarters. Each quarter should make three enchiladas.

Line a 9 x 13 pan with heavy duty aluminum foil, leaving 4-6 inches on each side to close it up. Brush 12 tortillas lightly with oil and microwave for 1 to 1 ½ minutes. Put 1/3 of the chicken mixture onto one side the tortilla and roll. Place into the pan.

After 12 tortillas are rolled, fold the sides of the foil up to the top of the pile the long way. Then fold the ends up to the center in a neat package. Put the package into the ice chest or the fridge.

Wash off the utensils and bowls and make another batch. Repeat until all enchiladas are rolled.

If you'd like, you can make up address labels with your contact information and attach them to the foil so that people can let you know if they're interested in re-ordering.

### Delivery

Put the enchiladas you are delivering into the ice chest. Staple your order form to a manila envelope and bring some change if possible. Make sure to start the deliveries early enough to be done before people start coming to pick up.

When you get to the house or the office, be sure to count the money and thank them for their order. Let them know that you will be doing this again in a few weeks and see if they're interested in re-ordering. Check off the order as paid and mark down if they want to order in the future.

Have fun!

### How to Make it Safe

Reinforce good hygiene practices before and during the cooking experience.

Watch your children while they are cooking on the stove.

Make sure food is refrigerated and stored properly.

Only sell to people you know or go door to door and into office buildings with your child.

### Phone Script

Hi my name is _____ from (however you know them). Is this a good time to talk? I'm doing a young entrepreneur project and I'm earning money for _____. I'm selling chicken and cheese enchiladas. These are not just plain cheese, like some schools sell. This is a family recipe that has been used for more than 30 years and they're really good. They are $15 per dozen and you can order them with or without onions. Which would you prefer? (Wait for them to answer) And how many dozen do you want? (Wait for them to answer) Thank you so much! These will be ready tomorrow after _____. What time do you want to pick them up or would you prefer delivery?

### Office Script

Hi, my name is _____ and I'm doing a young entrepreneur project. I'm earning money for

_____. I'm wondering if I can talk to the people in your office. (Wait for people to gather or go individually to each)

Hi, my name is _____ and I'm doing a young entrepreneur project. I'm earning money for

_____. I'm selling chicken and cheese enchiladas. These are not just plain cheese, like some schools sell. This is a family recipe that has been used for more than 30 years and they're really good. I'll deliver tomorrow by _____. They are $15 per dozen and you can order them with or without onions. I'll pass this form around. Please write down which would you prefer and how many dozen you want? (Have them write down the information.)

Is there someone that would be willing to hold the money for everyone in the office until I deliver them tomorrow? (Hand that person the envelope with the Office Order Form attached and ask them to paper clip cash for each order together.)

Thank you all so much! These will be delivered tomorrow after _____.

## Marketing Plan

The main method of marketing will be your child's own sales skills and referrals from previous customers. Have your child take their business cards with them and hand one out to each customer when they deliver their order.

Spread the word of your business to school mates, local businesses, your church congregation, relatives, neighbors, and friends. Keep your business cards and flyers handy to give out. Everyone needs to eat and your target market is nearly unlimited.

Be proactive and find new business opportunities. If your neighborhood is having a block party or your friends are planning a get-together, have your child offer the chicken enchiladas for sale. Are your neighbors going to have a big yard sale? Have your child bake several batches and offer them to hungry shoppers.

## Finances

The manila envelopes as suggested provide a good way to keep your child's earnings in one place.

At the end of the day, have your child count up their earnings by location. Help them keep track of the earnings in a spreadsheet or a manual table so they know how much they've made. This also helps your child determine which places are best to return to in the future and gives them a better idea of what customers to target.

Remind your child that their money will earn interest if they open a savings account at the bank and make regular deposits.

Try doing this business when chicken breasts are on sale to reduce the upfront costs and increase the profit margin.

If you provided the money for your child's supplies, have them repay you from the proceeds of the business. This will help your child learn responsibility. Also, have them save this same amount of money for the startup costs for next time.

*Jordan's Tip: You don't have to make enchiladas, especially if it's hard to find the ingredients in your town. You can also make sandwiches and chips, salads (green, chicken, egg), or wraps – perfect for the youngest cooks.*

## Chapter One: Know the Child

*"It is a wise father that knows his own child."* – William Shakespeare

Every child is different. Some are responsible and respectful from a very early age. Others need to be prodded to clean their room, do their homework, or perform weekly household chores. Each has certain strengths, and certain weaknesses. But no matter what type of personality your child has, there is no reason that he or she can't be successful as an entrepreneur.

There are no age limits, either. As we considered in the introductory chapter, your child's maturity is the number one factor in deciding whether he or she is ready to start their own business. Of course, you will want to take additional steps to keep pre-teens safe, but this does not restrict opportunity outside of capability and any special mental or physical challenges. Teenagers, with their more advanced ability to judge and a wider skill set, need little supervision.

The key to success is creating a balance between the level of maturity, age, personality, and skill set.

For the purposes of this book, we will look at children aged seven to seventeen, since this is the most common range of ages when kids are most ready to begin earning money.

Based on the Guerrilla Rainmaker DNA model I developed for adult entrepreneurs, I've used the same psychological constructs to explain the different business personalities that kids possess. The five major categories are Creator, Advancer, Refiner, Executor, and Flexer. We'll touch briefly on the most obvious and basic characteristics of each – since this is not a psychology text – but an understanding of the strengths and weaknesses associated with each role is important to develop a business plan personally geared toward your child.

*Creator*

In a nutshell, *Creators* are those who come up with new ideas and fresh concepts. They are stimulated by the fact that they live in a wide world of endless possibilities. These kids enjoy creative play activities that are unstructured and often get deeply involved in role-playing video games, fantasy novels, and art projects.

Many *Creators* are driven by feelings and relationships, instinct and intuition; logic is not a primary factor in their decision-making process. One of their core attributes is empathy toward others. The emotions of *Creators* run strong and tend to change without logical reason – driving their *Refiner* brothers or sisters crazy.

*Creators* need a positive outlet for their expression of emotion and can benefit from help staying on task. They tend to focus more on the potential of a plan rather than the realistic limitations. These children often become bored or impatient when their creativity is not adequately stimulated. They may be poorly prepared or disorganized when it comes to actually putting their business plan into action.

The personal strengths of *Creators* stem from their ability to explore alternatives when it comes to devising solutions to a problem. They can see the big picture and often challenge conventional thinking to bend existing rules or ignore standard methodology. *Creators* are the type of kids who really use their imagination to its full potential.

**Best Businesses for a Creator:** Chicken Enchilada Sales, Newsletter Writing, eBay Photography, Jewelry Making, and Mailbox Designs. *Creators* can look at a blank canvas and easily envision what embellishments are needed and explore ways to turn the ordinary into the extraordinary. Parents can help their *Creator* child by providing necessary structure.

## Advancer

The *Advancer* personality is one who thrives on communication. They enjoy taking ideas and carrying them forward, generating enthusiasm from others. Your *Advancer* child is most likely very gregarious and outgoing, making lots of friends quite easily. He or she is expressive and extroverted, attracting others with a strong desire to make a personal connection.

*Advancers* are great at selling and promoting. They are good at expressing themselves, yet sensitive to the needs of others, making them adept at networking and mingling in a group of strangers. *Advancers* tend to be fun and spirited and tend to bring those qualities to any job they do.

There's a flip side to those positive qualities of an *Advancer*, however. They can become frustrated by others who are not as attuned to emotional needs and tend to feel ignored or misunderstood often. Because he values cooperation and harmony, the *Advancer* child hates being in the middle of disagreements or having to be the bearer of bad news. If you are the parent of an *Advancer*, you may have been told by your child's teacher that she socializes too much during class.

I consider my oldest daughter, Jordan, to be the quintessential *Advancer*. She doesn't have any problem standing up in front of a crowd of strangers and speaking on business topics. Although she really enjoyed car washing and making enchiladas as a way to raise money, those businesses are not challenging enough to keep her interested and I expect her to move on to bigger and better enterprises. My youngest girl, Nyah, is following in her sister's footsteps. She is the life of the party and quite gregarious. I can see Nyah giving sports lessons due to her love of soccer and the playground.

**Best Businesses for an Advancer:** Babysitting, DJ, Candy Shop, Personal Shopper, Sports or Music Lessons. The *Advancer* is not afraid of public performances and their contagious enthusiasm makes them a natural to work with children or in sales. Parents can help *Advancers* promote their business by giving them ample opportunities to network.

## Refiner

The *Refiner* personality analyzes and challenges. They focus on the objective, analytical world of facts or theories, ideas or data. Their logical and systematic approach to problems make them ideal solvers who can be trusted to thoroughly examine a situation before moving forward – often viewed as a sign of maturity beyond their years. Emotions have no place in their decision-making model since they are wary of how this could cloud reason.

*Refiners* manage their time efficiently and can accomplish a lot in a day. They like to ask the question, "Why?" and want to hear a logical answer in response. *Refiner* kids love solving mysteries and playing games such as chess, which demand logical sequencing in order to win.

*Refiners* may feel threatened if someone else judges their efforts and finds them lacking. They have little respect for others, such as *Creators* and *Advancers,* who tend to use their emotions or gut instincts to make decisions. *Refiners* like to work by themselves, in isolation, and rarely communicate outside of what is necessary.

What *Refiners* are very good at is identifying anomalies and mistakes others have missed. Their forward thinking ability means they can predict surprises or complications before they occur. This results in a high degree of accuracy in nearly any activity.

My oldest boy, Sam, is a *Refiner*. He really enjoys logic, discussing the strangest things in order to delve deeper into a particular subject and analyze his own understanding. Sam tends to have a skeptical attitude, which his teachers don't always enjoy! Ben, my kindergartner, is showing signs of becoming a *Refiner* just like his older brother. He prefers to spend time alone and does not like it when others are watching his every move.

**Best Businesses for a Refiner:** Garage Cleaning, Car Wash, Green Housecleaning (they love experimenting with new formulas for cleaning products!), Computer Repair, and Pool Maintenance. Because the *Refiner* child prefers working solo, these are all ideal businesses. Their ability to delve into the root of a problem makes them a natural at troubleshooting and finding new ways of using technology to reach goals. Parents of *Refiners* should encourage these kids to step out of their comfort zone in order to promote their business. If you exhibit a lot of enthusiasm, it will give your *Refiner* the necessary confidence to succeed.

## Executor

*Executors* are the most realistic and detail-oriented of all the personality types. If you have an *Executor* child in your family, you surely realize they have a great need for structure and organization. These kids don't give up easily. They take pride in their accomplishments and the ability to complete projects. Their style is very practical and systematic.

Due to their focus on reality, *Executors* are often viewed as inflexible or close-minded. They tend to be impatient and want immediate results – although they don't like to feel pushed or rushed. *Executors* are not likely to take risks, preferring traditional methodology.

*Executors* have a lot of great talents. They enjoy keeping track of the little details that others gloss over. They enjoy routine tasks and a schedule that doesn't vary too much. They do communicate clearly and concisely with others – but only join in the conversation if it pertains to their personal experiences. *Executors* are great at planning and organizing.

When it comes to my family, my second daughter, Taylor, is the *Executor* of the bunch. She is very organized and addicted to structure, always stressing about being on time. Her attention to detail makes her an excellent student who gets good grades. Taylor makes money by cleaning my suite of offices – a job which really suits her desire to deliver concrete results and gives her a sense of accomplishment.

**Best Businesses for an Executor:** Garage Organizing, Party Helper or Planner, Lawn Care, and Window or Car Washing. Although they don't want to be rushed, they take the time to plan the details of each task in advance and enjoy the repetition of unimaginative work. Parents can help their *Executor* children excel in any business by encouraging conceptual thinking, imagination, and a focus on the bigger picture.

## Flexer

Kids that are very well-rounded and enjoy a variety of different types of pursuits can be categorized as *Flexers*. These children don't exhibit a real affinity for any particular role, enjoying a combination of traits and motivators. They are true adapters who can recognize and relate to the perspectives of *Creators, Advancers, Refiners,* and *Executors.*

If you are the parent of a true *Flexer*, count yourself lucky. These kids can excel at nearly anything they put their mind to. Encourage them to find their passion and then step back!

Not every kid is going to fit neatly into these categories, but it is helpful to identify those common traits which shape their behavior. Once you know their personality style, you will be better equipped to help your children find a business they enjoy – and that is the key to motivating kids to stick with the plan and achieve success.

It is likely that your child's personality also influences their skills. A *Refiner* kid is probably a whiz at putting together an Erector set while an *Executor* child most likely organizes their closet and dresser drawers by color and style. While they are two different personalities, each kid brings his or her own set of strengths and talents to any business they might choose.

I'm hoping that my two youngest sons, Tommy and Gabe, will fill the void in my family by growing up to be true *Creators*. Then again, they could turn out to be *Flexers* as a result of having so many siblings as role models. But no matter what roles my youngest kids step into, I'll be there to support them and do my best to understand their unique personalities.

Remember that you need to combine your own child's core attributes with his or her age to find an appropriate entrepreneurial opportunity. All of the business plans included in this book include a range of ages which I consider to be suitable for the tasks involved.

Here are two more business plans you might want to consider for your son or daughter. The candy shop business and DJ service are perfect fits for your *Creator* or *Flexer* children.

## Business Plan for a Candy Shop

### General Description

This business is perfect for kids aged: 7 – 17 years old

**Mission Statement**: To provide a neighborhood or event 'store' with candy kids can afford to buy.

**Goals and Objectives**: The goal is to create a business that provides a good source of income by working weekends, afternoons, and nights at events throughout the year. The objective is to compete with other vendors by offering popular candy and drinks at a low price.

**Business Philosophy**: Making it easy for kids to buy the candy, ice cream, and drinks they want.

**Marketing**: Work with event coordinators, yard sales, coaches, etc. to be approved for selling at various venues throughout the year. Hand out business cards wherever appropriate to find future opportunities.

Competitive strengths are the low prices and convenience of this candy shop.

The pricing structure will vary by the cost of goods sold but generally will start at $0.25 and go on up to $1.50 per item (easily affordable for kids with an allowance).

**What this business teaches** – How to make change, sales, planning in advance, customer service.

### Operational Plan

**Inventory: What You'll Need**

- Candy
- Laffy Taffy
- Tic-Tacs
- Snickers
- Twix
- Milky Way

- o Hot Tamales
- o Nerds
- o Hershey Bar
- o Three Musketeers
- o M&Ms
- o Skittles
- o Starburst
- o Butterfinger
- o 100 Grand
- o Big Hunk
- o Heath Bar
- o Reese's
- o Baby Ruth
- o Pay Day
- o Airheads
- o Sugar Daddies
- o Dots
- o Almond Joy
- o Red Hots
- o Tootsie Pops
- o Licorice
- o Gummy bears
- o Lemon Heads
- o Tootsie Rolls
- o Mr. Goodbar
- o Altoids
- o Life Savers
- o Chiclets
- o Junior Mints
- o Now & Laters
- o Kit Kat
- o Mounds
- o Milk Duds
- o Sweet Tarts
- o Bit-o-Honey
- o Blow Pops
- o Jolly Ranchers
- o Crunch Bar
- o Pop Tarts

- Ice cream bars, Otter Pops, ice cream sandwiches, etc.
- Gum
- Pop, Gatorade, Powerade, hot chocolate (if the weather is cold), etc.
- Water, Vitamin Water, etc.
- Ice Chest
- 10-20 lbs crushed or block ice
- Card table
- Folding Chair
- Money box or envelope
- Change
- Ice cream bars, Otter Pops, ice cream sandwiches, etc.
- Gum

- Pop, Gatorade, Powerade, hot chocolate (if the weather is cold), etc.
- Water, Vitamin Water, etc.
- Ice Chest
- 10-20 lbs crushed or block ice
- Card table
- Folding Chair
- Money box or envelope
- Change
- Price Signs
- Candy List (optional)

**What You Do – Preparation**

Think about where you're going to set up your candy shop. It can be anywhere that people are going to get thirsty or hungry but don't want to or can't leave. Sporting events and garage sales are great because people usually don't think about bringing something to eat or drink, but they get hot and hungry.

Purchase your supplies. Make sure you store the drinks and ice cream in a deep freezer so that they stay frozen hard until you take them to the event. Take the drinks out an hour or so before the event so that they will be somewhat thawed by the time you get there.

Think about how you are going to price your candy. If you buy it in bulk, you can buy it pretty inexpensively. You may want to price it reasonably low so that you'll have a lot of volume. It's good to have some candy priced at $0.25, $0.50, $1.00, and $1.50. This way, different kids in the same family will buy their own candy and people will buy more than one at a time.

Print up the price signs. Use a standard font like Times New Roman and a size of 275 points to create one sign per price. They are large so that you can put each one in front of a section of candy that is all one price. You may also want to print the customized list with the price of each. Think about what you're saving the money for so you can tell people if they ask.

Load up all your candy in a box and put the drinks and ice cream into the cooler with the ice. If it's hot in your area, you may consider putting the candy bars that might melt into the cooler too.

Make sure you get to the event early so that you can set up at a prime location. This is going to be where people are entering and exiting the event and can see you easily.

### What You Do – On the Job

Have fun! Smile and talk to people as they go by. Let them know what you're selling. Be sure to save money from your sales to repay the upfront costs of the supplies and to replenish them.

### How to Make it Safe

Parents, be within eyesight of your child in case they don't know how to answer a question and to ensure that they are safe.

### Price List

You can print this list out as is or put it into an Excel spreadsheet.

| | Price | | Price | | Price |
|---|---|---|---|---|---|
| 100 Grand | | KitKat | | Starburst | |
| Airheads | | Laffy Taffy | | Sugar Daddies | |
| Almond Joy | | Lemon Heads | | Sweet Tarts | |
| Altoids | | Licorice | | Three Musketeers | |
| Baby Ruth | | Life Savers | | Tic-Tacs | |
| Big Hunk | | M&Ms | | Tootsie Pops | |
| Bit-o-Honey | | Milk Duds | | Tootsie Rolls | |
| Blow Pops | | Milky Way | | Twix | |
| Butterfinger | | Mounds | | Ice Cream sandwiches | |
| Chicklets | | Mr. Goodbar | | Ice Cream Bars | |
| Crunch Bar | | Nerds | | Otter Pops | |
| Dots | | Now & Laters | | Gum | |
| Gummy Bears | | Pay Day | | Soda | |
| Heath Bar, | | Pop Tarts | | Gatorade | |
| Hershey Bar | | Red Hots | | Powerade | |
| Hot Tamales | | Reese's | | Hot Chocolate | |
| Jolly Ranchers | | Skittles | | Water | |
| Junior Mints | | Snickers | | Vitamin Water | |

## Marketing Plan

Marketing will start by contacting the people in charge of various events and venues, such as coaches for team sports, neighbors holding yard sales, business owners, etc. Pay attention to signs in your neighborhood advertising upcoming events and activities and write down the phone number to call the person in charge. It is best to contact as many people in advance as possible in order to create an appointment calendar for the next several months. Always check with the event coordinator if it is okay to set up your shop; some towns and organizations have strict laws regarding where and what you can sell.

Remember to keep your business cards handy at all times. Give them out to your customers and anyone you encounter at stores, school, church, etc. who might have need of your candy shop at their next event.

Online marketing is also appropriate. Post to your Facebook and/or Twitter account that you are now the proud owner of your own business. Ask your friends and followers to notify you of any upcoming events where you could set up shop.

*Finances*

Keep track of inventory cost and your earnings in a spreadsheet or a manual table so you know how much you can earn, and how much you have made, at various activities and events. When you review this table later you can easily see which types of events are most profitable – and which are probably not worth your time.

Purchase your supplies when they are on sale or go to a warehouse club to get the best price. It's a good idea to buy packages that have a variety of candies so that you don't have to buy as many. It might be cheaper to order candy in bulk online, especially if you don't have a big warehouse or discount store in your town. Dollar stores are good choices, too.

Your money will earn interest if you open a savings account at the bank and make regular deposits.

If your parents provided the money for the cost of your initial inventory, consider paying them back from the proceeds of your business. They are sure to be impressed by your responsibility. Remember to set aside some of your proceeds to pay for more inventory as necessary so you don't have to ask your parents for money again.

*Jordan's Tip: If kids in your area really like a particular type of candy (the kids in my neighborhood really like Mexican lemon salt), make sure to keep lots of it in stock.*

## Business Plan for a Party DJ

### *General Description*

This business is perfect for kids aged: 13 – 17 years old

**Mission Statement**: To provide entertainment for special occasions.

**Goals and Objectives**: The goal is to create a part-time business that provides a good source of income by working weekends, afternoons, and nights as available throughout the year. The objective is to build a business that can expand and extend into college years, while building a reputation for reliability, personalized customer service, and professionalism.

**Business Philosophy**: To become the community/neighborhood source for entertainment.

**Marketing**: This service will be marketed to neighbors, friends, church members, and extended family members who are planning a celebration for a special occasion such as a birthday party, neighborhood block party, or sports team victory event.

Competitive strengths are the cost, availability, and reliability of the service.

Pricing structure varies according to location and the duration of each event, but should be well below the professional DJ rate.

**What this business teaches** – Responsibility, reliability, how to create/maintain inventory, how to organize, how to service a diverse demographic.

### *Operational Plan*

**Inventory: What You'll Need**

- Tabletop stereo system, or iPod with speakers
- Karaoke machine (optional)

- Turntable, mixer, headphones (optional)
- A wide assortment of music genres in mp3 or CD format
- Extension cord(s)
- Disco ball (optional)
- Fun lighting, such as strobes (optional)

**What You Do – Preparation**

Practice with your friends first. Invite them over for a small party and provide the music. This is a good way to start because you already know the genre of music they prefer. The key is putting tunes together in a pleasing manner; don't play a hard rock song followed by a slow country ballad. Try to get your friends up and moving, dancing, and having a good time. Tell stories or talk about music trivia in between sets and get them excited to hear the next song.

Plan your sets. Develop blocks of songs with a similar theme, beat, or rhythm. Record and keep the lists in a notebook so you know ahead of time what music you will be playing and have sets of comparable length and style.

Use iTunes software or something similar to transfer songs to a CD. This will also let you see how long each set is, time wise.

If you are using a karaoke machine, print up a list of the available songs and keep that in a separate binder so guests can page through it. You will also need postcards or a notebook where they can indicate their song choice and be placed in the waiting line.

Since you are just starting out, you will need to charge less than DJs with lots of experience and fancy equipment. Come up with an hourly rate based on what others in your community are charging, then divide that by half. You could also charge a set fee for a job up to four hours.

You may want to get a container, such as a large tote or plastic tub, to put all of your equipment, notebooks, and music in. This will make it easier to transport. The place where you are performing should provide a table and chair for you to set up; if not you will have to invest in a folding table and chair to bring with you.

Make up flyers that include your name, the days and hours you're available, the type of equipment you are using along with any optional extras, your contact information, and your rate of pay. Specify the types of music you have in your inventory such as rock, alternative, etc. Make the flyers professional but fun. Add some graphics like music notes, clip art of people dancing, etc.

When you get a call for a job from someone you don't personally know, find out how they heard about you. Make sure to get their name, address, and phone number.

When you take a job, find out how many people are expected to attend the event, what hours you'll be working, when you can start setting up your equipment, and if they'll be providing transportation.

### What You Do – On the Job

Find a corner of the main room or outdoor space to set up your equipment. You don't want to be in the middle of the flow of traffic, but you do want people to see you so they know where to put in song requests. If you are using lights or a disco ball, ask the customer about they would prefer you to set it up. You may need help finding electrical outlets and hanging lights.

Match the music to the event. If it's a child's birthday

party, for instance, you will want to play songs the kids can understand and that are popular with that particular age group.

Take a break between sets. Let prearranged music play while you get a drink and relax for a few minutes.

You may want to keep a good supply of bottled water in a small ice chest nearby to make it easy to stay hydrated while you're working.

At the end of your gig, pack up your equipment and leave the area neat and clean. Before you leave, ask for a referral from your customer.

### How to Make It Safe

Parents, don't let your child accept any jobs where there will only be adults at the event or if alcohol will be served.

Go with your child to the event and check it out beforehand to ensure that it is a safe environment. Offer to help with electrical connections and setup.

## Marketing Plan

The main methods of marketing will be word of mouth, referrals, and flyers posted in your neighborhood. At the end of each DJ gig, offer business cards that your satisfied clients can share with other people they know.

Spread the word of your business to school mates, your church congregation, relatives, neighbors, and friends. Keep your business cards and flyers handy at all times to give out when the opportunity presents itself. Keep an eye out for notice of special events in your community or neighborhood; be proactive about getting work by approaching the organizers and offering your services.

Online marketing is good, too. Post to your Facebook and/or Twitter account that you are now the proud owner of your own business. Let your friends and followers know you are available for DJ jobs but don't post the specifics of where you will be on your next gig. Ask your friends and followers to notify you of any upcoming events where your services might be needed.

## Finances

Expect satisfied customers to give you a tip if they think you have done an exceptional job – and congratulate yourself on exceeding your customers' expectations. You can also place a small tip jar on your table while working; most people will add to it when they request a song.

Keep track of your earnings in a spreadsheet or a manual table so you know how much you can earn, and how much you have made. Be sure to include the amount of any tips – these are customers you will want to go out of your way to work for again and again.

Your money will earn interest if you open a savings account at the bank and make regular deposits.

Parents, if you provided the money for the equipment, have your child pay you back from the first proceeds of their business. When your child has made a profit, they might want to reinvest the money back into the business by buying new or additional equipment in order to expand – especially if this is a business they want to keep in the future.

***Jordan's Tip:*** *Collect lots of different music, even if you don't personally like it, in order to have something for everyone.*

## Chapter Two: Finding the Right Motivators

*"A burning desire is the greatest **motivator** of every human action. The desire for success implants 'success consciousness' which, in turn, creates a vigorous and ever-increasing 'habit of success'."* – Paul J. Meyer, The Leading Edge Publishing Company

Can any business be successful without motivation? For adults, our motivators are pretty simple to figure out; essentials for our household and support of our families usually rank pretty high on the list.

Every kid has something they want. Some of those wants are more frivolous than others. For example, being the first one in a group of friends to own the latest video game or a new pair of shoes from the mall that *everyone* else is wearing are items with fleeting value. But in today's materialistic society our kids are inundated with messages about what's cool to wear, what's exciting to play, what's the best way to be entertained. This superficial commercialism does nothing to help our kids grow and mature.

On the other hand, there are many worthwhile pursuits your child is probably interested in, too. Saving for college, playing a team sport or musical instrument, or developing a constructive hobby are all things that cost money but most parents would consider them a good use of a savings account. I encourage all of my kids to participate in sports because I believe any type of physical activity teaches them discipline, how to get along with others, how to be part of a team, and keeps their minds sharp even in the summer months. If any of them want to pursue sports past the intermediate level, I will do everything possible to show them how they can reach their goals through hard work.

As a parent who wants to teach your children constructive life and business skills, it is important to positively influence the choices they make. Before your child starts his or her own business, you need to help him decide on the motivator that will get him through the tough times and keep him engaged in earning an income.

As I previously related, my daughter Jordan's motivator was a trip to New York to attend the NSA Youth Conference. Was I lucky that my daughter's goal was such a constructive one? Well, yes and no. I am very proud of her, but I also made sure that she was raised with good morals, standards, and ethics.

Don't get me wrong. I'm not asking you to name me Father of the Year. I made my share of mistakes along the way; we all do. But I can't stress to you enough the importance of focusing on the positive things you want your child to become now. Right now.

Many parents give their kids everything they want. They may do so out of guilt, out of fear, or due to a misplaced notion that they must provide everything they didn't get during their own childhood. It may make the adults feel better temporarily, but it doesn't do anything to develop their children's positive attributes.

Forget about the goals you want your child to have. Just because you always dreamed of being a bestselling author doesn't mean your child shares the same vision. Your young entrepreneur is not going to be motivated by your concept of an ideal life goal. I have to remind myself of this concept often; even though I have seven chances of seeing one of my kids follow in their father's footsteps, I can't force them to do it.

Kids and teens need to personally identify the goal they are trying to achieve before they become an entrepreneur. Not only is it helpful to keep this goal in mind as they wash a car or mow a lawn, it should be communicated to the people they are serving. This makes it more real to the kids, as well as providing a worthwhile reason for customers to help. What person could say no to a child who is motivated enough to go out and raise money for his college education?

This is one of the reasons we provide a script with business plans, as appropriate. Simply asking a neighbor or friend to perform work in exchange for money isn't nearly as effective as a kid explaining her ultimate goal and how she hopes to achieve it.

I encourage you to sit down with your child right now and discuss the things most important to them in the future. Not the latest techno-gadget or toy, but those things that will make a positive impact on their future. Start a one-on-one conversation and actually listen to what your son or daughter is saying.

If your child is having a hard time focusing on the future, you may have to remind him of the immediate rewards of working. Parents know about the intangible rewards, such as responsibility, financial savvy, and others, but kids – especially younger ones – will be more motivated by tangible incentives. Strike up a deal with your child; say, for every $100 they earn, they get to spend $10 of it on something they want now. The rest should go into a savings or checking account.

In fact, the act of opening a bank account often functions as a motivator in and of itself. Younger kids feel more grown up when they hold a savings account book in their hands. Each time they enter the bank and make a deposit, they see the balance grow and it alerts them to the greater possibilities of what that money can provide.

Teens are different, of course. Their "big ticket" goals are more immediate, such as buying a car, paying for the first semester at a university, or getting a new laptop that will help them write a lengthy research report. Older kids can be trusted with a checking account and debit card. This shows them that you trust them enough to give them additional fiscal responsibility. Do stress that their ultimate goal will never be achieved if they spend the money on pizza or a shopping trip to the mall. Help them keep their goal in mind in order to resist those immediate wants that often trump their future needs.

Make the process of starting a business fun. The exercises I have created – great for the whole family to get involved in – are meant to be a fun way to learn business. I include some sample exercises in Chapter Five, but you can find many more online when you start a membership at Cash Club for Kids.

Here are another two business plans, one for coaching sports and one for teaching music lessons. Both of these businesses are longer term than some others, so they will require that your child stay focused on the goal and motivated to complete each block of lessons.

## Business Plan for Sports Coaching

### *General Description*

This business is perfect for kids aged: 13 – 17 years old

**Mission Statement:** To teach kids how to play a sport safely but competitively.

**Goals and Objectives:** The goal is to create a part-time business that provides a good source of income by working weekends, afternoons, and nights as available throughout the year. The objective is to form a business that provides a valuable service, while building a reputation for safety, reliability and professionalism.

**Business Philosophy:** To become the community/neighborhood source for teaching sports skills.

**Marketing:** This service will be marketed to neighbors, friends, church members, and extended family members who have school-aged children interested in sports or already playing in a league.

Competitive strengths are the cost, availability, and reliability of the service.

The pricing structure will be an hourly rate, but should be well below the professional instructor's rate.

**What this business teaches:** Responsibility, reliability, customer service, teaching skills, patience.

### *Operational Plan*

#### Inventory: What You'll Need

- Your own sports equipment

- o Soccer balls
- o Baseballs/bats/gloves
- o Football
- o Volleyball
- o Basketball/hoop
- o Skateboard
- o Bicycle
- Items that can be used to mark off a field, serve as goals or nets, etc.
- Cones
- Safety equipment
- Knee, elbow or shin pads
- Goggles
- Clothing
- Workout wear
- Appropriate shoes
- Athletic cup (boys)
- Helmet
- Stopwatch/timer
- Bottled water
- Lesson plan
- Yard or field of appropriate size
- CPR and first aid lessons/certification (see Chapter Seven: Resources)
- First aid kit

**What You Do – Preparation**

First, find a place where lessons can be held. This might be in your backyard, your school recess area after hours, the YMCA, or a public sports field or park. Just be sure that it will always be available at the times you schedule lessons. Some sports, such as basketball, racquetball, or swimming will obviously require a location with the right equipment already in place.

Plan out your lessons before-hand then decide how much time is required to effectively teach a child how to play a sport or to play it more competitively. This might be once a week for several months.

Plan a time period convenient for several children so you can teach a group rather than just an individual child. This works best for team sports but not so well for sports like swimming, skateboarding or other individual sports that require you to keep a close eye on the student.

Create a schedule on a calendar. If you are giving individual weekly lessons, you probably won't have time to work with more than one or two students at a time. Plan for family vacations and other times you won't be available and make up for that hole by adding a lesson to the end of the block.

Print up flyers that include your name, the days and hours you're available, the type of sports you are teaching along with your contact information (phone number and email address only), and your rate of pay. Make the flyers professional but fun. Add some graphics like sports equipment, clip art of people playing, etc.

When you get a job from someone you don't personally know, find out how they heard about you. Make sure to get their name, address, and phone number. Ask them where they expect the lessons to take place and if they will provide transportation.

## What You Do – On the Job

Get the field of play set up with goals, nets, boundaries, etc. You might have to walk off distances, or use a long measuring tape to get the proper size.

Ensure that your student is wearing the appropriate gear to stay safe. If not, speak with the parents about the importance of providing the right apparel and accessories. Ask them to purchase the necessities and don't start lessons until the child is wearing them.

It is up to you to make sure the child you are teaching stays focused and pays attention to the lesson. Be creative; make it fun. If you are putting the student through a timed drill, for instance, you might want to bring along a portable music system and play a song. Ask the child to keep going until the music ends.

Each child will learn at their own rate. Adjust your lessons to match the child's ability level and talent.

If you are working with a group, make sure that everyone gets a chance to play various positions and use all the equipment. Encourage kids who are struggling; don't allow others to make fun of them.

Take a short break midway through the lesson.

Both you and your student need to stay hydrated – make sure there is always fresh water available. If it is really hot, limit lessons to shorter time periods and ensure there is shade nearby where everyone can rest.

Keep an eye out for any signs of physical distress. Stop the lesson immediately if you feel the student(s) is in any sort of danger.

At the end of the lesson, pack up your equipment and leave the area neat and clean.

You may want to present a certificate of completion/achievement at the end of the course of lessons. It can easily be created using your computer and printer and a form you can buy, or simply printed on a colored sheet of paper listing the course name, the child's name, the date, and a signature line for you.

### How to Make it Safe

Parents, accompany your child to each lesson. Keep an eye out for brewing fights, signs of physical distress, injury, or any other danger. Have your cell phone handy.

## Marketing Plan

The main methods of marketing will be word of mouth, referrals, and flyers posted in your neighborhood. You can also approach any players on school or community teams and ask if they would like extra, individualized lessons. Give them one of your business cards to take home to their parents. Ask your local sporting goods store if you can post a flyer on their bulletin board.

Spread the word of your business to school mates, your church congregation, relatives, neighbors, and friends. Keep your business cards and flyers handy at all times to give out when the opportunity presents itself.

Online marketing is good, too. Post to your Facebook and/or Twitter account that you are now the proud owner of your own business. Let your friends and followers know you are available for sports lessons and ask them for leads, but don't post the specifics of your address.

## Finances

Provide a payment plan for your customers – either payment at the end of each lesson or a monthly amount that can be collected beforehand. Expect satisfied customers to give you a tip if they think you have done an exceptional job – and congratulate yourself on exceeding your customers' expectations.

It may be more convenient for some customers to pay you with a check. Ask your parents if they will help you cash the checks at the bank or set up your own account so you can deposit them.

This is a business you can continue throughout school and even during college. If so, you will want to reinvest some of your earnings in additional or upgraded equipment.

***Jordan's Tip:*** *Stay on top of your game during your spare time – the better you get, the better you can teach others.*

## Business Plan for
## Musical/Singing Lessons

*General Description*

This business is perfect for kids aged: 12 – 17 years old

**Mission Statement**: To teach kids how to play an instrument or sing.

**Goals and Objectives**: The goal is to create a part-time business that provides a good source of income by working weekends, afternoons, and nights as available throughout the year. The objective is to form a business that can expand and extend into college years, while building a reputation for reliability and professionalism.

**Business Philosophy**: To become the community/neighborhood source for teaching kids interested in learning music or advancing their skills.

**Marketing**: This service will be marketed to neighbors, friends, church members, and extended family members who have school-aged children interested in music.

Competitive strengths are the cost, availability, and reliability of the service.

The pricing structure will be an hourly rate, but should be well below the professional instructor's rate.

**What this business teaches** – Responsibility, reliability, customer service, teaching skills, patience.

*Operational Plan*

**Inventory: What You'll Need**

- Your own instrument
- Karaoke machine with microphone (optional for singing lessons)
- Electronic or manual tuner
- Sheet music
- Music stand
- Lesson plan
- Homework assignments

**What You Do – Preparation**

Come up with a standard lesson package; say once a week, for an hour at a time, for a six-month period.

Create a lesson plan for the beginning musician or singer. You may need to adjust this after you begin working with each student to match the child's skill level. Some kids will learn quickly while others will have a harder time. Organize your lessons in a three-ring binder so they are easy to transport.

Make assignments for the student to complete on his or her own each week. Provide a student folder where they can keep their weekly homework assignments.

Make copies of the songs you will be teaching so the student can have his own copy in front of him while learning.

Figure out where to hold lessons. It may be a spare room in your home or you could offer to teach at the student's house if it is someone you know well who lives nearby. Of course, if you are teaching piano lessons, you will have to give lessons at your house, unless the student has his or her own piano at home. Remember the noise factor; try to find a spot that won't disturb others.

Create a schedule on a calendar. If you are giving

weekly lessons, you probably won't have time to work with more than one or two students at a time. Plan for family vacations, holidays, and other times you won't be available.

Make up flyers that include your name, the days and hours you're available, the type of instruments/music you are teaching along with your contact information (phone number and email address only), and your rate of pay. Make the flyers professional but fun. Add some graphics like music notes, clip art of people playing an instrument, etc.

When you get a job from someone you don't personally know, find out how they heard about you. Make sure to get their name, address, and phone number. Ask them where they expect the lessons to take place and if they will provide transportation.

### What You Do – On the Job

Set up your music stand, stool (if needed), and sheet music – or karaoke machine if you are giving singing lessons. Get the student situated with his own instrument and sheet music.

Do some warm-up exercises before going into the lesson.

It is up to you to make sure the child you are teaching stays focused and pays attention to the lesson. Be creative; make it fun; teach the kind of music the child likes best.

Each child will learn at their own rate. Adjust your lessons to match the child's ability level and talent.

Test the student each week on what they learned in the previous lesson. Enlist the parent's help ensuring that homework assignments are done; ask the parent to sign off on completion.

At the end of the lesson, pack up your equipment and leave the area neat and clean.

### How to Make It Safe

Parents, accompany your child to the first lesson or two outside your home to ensure it is a safe environment.

## *Marketing Plan*

The main methods of marketing will be word of mouth, referrals, and flyers posted in your neighborhood. You can also approach any beginning band students in your school and ask if they would like lessons. Give them one of your business cards to take home to their parents. Ask your local music store if you can post a flyer on their bulletin board.

Spread the word of your business to school mates, your church congregation, relatives, neighbors, and friends. Keep your business cards and flyers handy at all times to give out when the opportunity presents itself.

Online marketing is good, too. Post to your Facebook and/or Twitter account that you are now the proud owner of your own business. Let your friends and followers know you are available for music lessons but don't post the specifics of your address.

## *Finances*

Provide a payment plan for your customers – either payment at the end of each lesson or a monthly amount with specific due date (either payable in advance or at the last lesson of the month). Expect satisfied customers to give you a tip if they think you have done an exceptional job – and congratulate yourself on exceeding your customers' expectations.

It may be more convenient for some customers to pay you with a check. Ask your parents if they will help you cash the checks at the bank or set up your own account so you can deposit them.

This is a business you can continue throughout school and even during college. If so, you will want to reinvest some of your earnings in additional or upgraded equipment.

*Jordan's Tip: Keep practicing your instrument at home – the better you get, the better you can teach others.*

## Chapter Three: Making Plans

*"Before everything else, getting ready is the secret of success."* – Henry Ford

Most of us know the importance of having a plan in place before starting a new business. But it's even more vital for the young entrepreneur to develop a written plan since she doesn't have any prior experience.

The plan should include time frames, goals, and a step-by-step guide to everything that needs to be accomplished. Although I've provided you with lots of prepared business plans in this book, this process will allow you to easily create your own, or tweak these to personalize the details for your child based on his or her personality, age, maturity level, and skills.

One thing I did not include in my business plans for your kids and teens is a time frame. It is up to you to decide how many hours or days your child has to comfortably devote to a business. Some kids are very involved in extracurricular activities throughout the school year, limiting the time available for other pursuits. It may be that weekends fit best in your schedule, as well as your child's. Then again, some kids might only have the summer months to work at their business. But no matter your personal circumstances, it is important to add dates to each specific goal, otherwise they tend to get swallowed up by more immediate needs and nothing gets accomplished.

For instance, start with the supplies needed. You may need to purchase cleaning products, paper for flyers, or findings to make jewelry. Make each of these a short-term goal, and add a due date. Create another to-do item, such as creating and printing flyers. The next item might be posting those flyers around the neighborhood. Depending on the type of business your child chooses, they may also need to delegate time to practice their skills or create inventory. When you've got a time frame to accomplish all these little details, it will give you a clearer idea of what day your child will be available for that first job.

We talked about long-term goals in depth in the last chapter. In regards to your child's personalized business plan, you will need to add short-term goals, as well, along with a due date. It is much easier for a kid to work toward that long-term goal if it is broken down into smaller, more manageable guideposts.

Let's imagine that your teen's ultimate goal is to raise enough money for the first two semesters of college. The cost is $10,000. That's a pretty hefty amount. Remember that old question, "How do you eat an elephant?" The answer is, "One bite at a time." This certainly applies to such a large goal.

Try breaking it down into increments of $1,000. Perhaps it will take three months to achieve this first, shorter-term goal. This is a comfortable time frame, but the need might be more urgent. It will help motivate your teen to stay on track if he or she aims to make that amount in one month during the summer, when more work time is available. This is still doable, but creates a greater sense of urgency.

If your child has a year or more to work towards the ultimate goal, this month-to-month breakdown makes it achievable. A "sales and income forecast" added to the business plan might look something like this:

| INCOME | Jan | Feb | Mar | Apr | May | Jun | Jul | Aug | Sep | Oct | Nov | Dec | Total annual $ |
|---|---|---|---|---|---|---|---|---|---|---|---|---|---|
| NET INCOME | $500 | $500 | $500 | $500 | $750 | $1,000 | $1,000 | $1,000 | $1,000 | $750 | $500 | $250 | $8,250 |
| EXPENSES | Jan | Feb | March | April | May | June | July | Aug | Sep | Oct | Nov | Dec | Total annual $ |
| Supplies | $50 | $50 | $50 | $50 | $75 | $100 | $100 | $100 | $75 | $50 | $50 | $25 | $775 |
| Gas/Transportation | $0 | $0 | $0 | $0 | $0 | $0 | $0 | $0 | $0 | $0 | $0 | $0 | $0 |
| TOTAL Expenses | $50 | $50 | $50 | $50 | $75 | $100 | $100 | $100 | $75 | $50 | $50 | $25 | $775 |
| Cash left over | $450 | $450 | $450 | $450 | $675 | $900 | $900 | $900 | $925 | $700 | $450 | $225 | $7,475 |

This spreadsheet shows that the teen will be three quarters of the way to the ultimate goal within a twelve-month period when working on their business monthly. As each small goal is achieved, it provides the necessary motivation to reach that $10,000 without losing hope.

Don't forget to plan for "off" time, too. This example projection shows a very low sales figure for the month of December, a time period typically full of holiday parties and events. Schedule in family vacations, too. Create a good balance between work and fun.

The younger the entrepreneur, the more time should be allocated for activities with family and friends, hobbies, and extracurricular pursuits such as sports or band practice. It may be that a child younger than ten will only earn a couple hundred dollars through their business venture but that's all right; the point is to teach the necessary skills and business acumen rather than creating a self-made millionaire before reaching adolescence.

At this point, the important business objectives are still rather vague. We have a timeline and the amount of money that needs to be earned, but there is no step-by-step plan in place to make it happen. Now we need to drill down into the specific details that will allow this to happen.

Some things you can add to the business plan:

- Further marketing and promotional ideas
- Advertising (low- or no-cost) such as a classified ad in the local Penny Saver paper, online bulletin boards, etc.
- Ways to increase sales, such as related products, or packaging
- Pricing strategy
- Group services that pay more than individual lessons
- Ways to beat the competition

Spend some time brainstorming these ideas and concepts. After the business has been in place for a couple months, go back and fine tune those ideas to better fit with the factors your child has experienced thus far. A business plan, and in particular, a marketing strategy, is always a work in progress rather than a static document.

Remember the famous words of Napoleon Hill, author of *Think and Grow Rich*, "A goal is a dream with a deadline."

In the next chapter we will take a more in-depth look at the "real" aspects of running a business, such as determining return on investment and creating a budget.

For now, I'll leave you with two more business plans. These are for a babysitting and pet washing service that require only simple supplies but a good level of maturity.

## Business Plan for a Babysitting Service

### *General Description*

This business is perfect for kids aged: 11 – 17 years old

**Mission Statement**: To provide reliable, trustworthy babysitting service for parents with young children.

**Goals and Objectives**: The goal is to create a business that provides a good source of income by working weekends, afternoons, and nights throughout the year. The objective is to build a reputation for trustworthiness and obtain repeat clientele.

**Business Philosophy**: To become the babysitter parents can trust.

**Marketing**: This service will be marketed to neighbors, friends, church members, and extended family members with young children.

Competitive strengths are the honesty, reliability, and trustworthiness of the babysitter.

Pricing structure varies according to location and competition.

**What this business teaches** – Responsibility, child care, the importance of being punctual.

### *Operational Plan*

#### Inventory: What You'll Need

- CPR and First Aid training (optional but highly recommended)
- Babysitting training class (optional but

recommended)
- List of emergency numbers in your area
- Fun Bag or Box
- Age appropriate movies
- Crayons, Coloring Books
- Stickers, Card games (Uno, Go Fish, etc.)
- Crafts
- Candy (if allowed)
- Colored paper and a printer

**What You Do – Preparation**

It's important to get the proper training like you would with any other business. Consider taking a CPR, First Aid, or babysitting class through your local Red Cross or Parks and Recreation department. This will help you feel more comfortable if you've never babysat before and will be a selling point for the parents.

There's no set rate to charge for sitting, so find out what the going rate is for babysitting in your area. Ask your parents, friends, or relatives who babysit what they charge. You may consider lowering your rate if there's a lot of competition for babysitting or you may charge the same rate but include light housekeeping at no charge.

Put together your fun bag. Make sure to include things that are appropriate for all ages.

Make up flyers that include your name, the days and hours you're available, your experience level and training, references, your contact information, and your rate of pay if you have a set amount. If you're going to do light housekeeping, add this as well. Make it professional but fun. Also include that you have fun activities for kids of all ages. Hand these out to people you know from church, your younger siblings' friends, your parent's friends, and people in the neighborhood.

When you get a job, find out how they heard about you if you don't personally know them. Make sure to get their name, address, and phone number. Also find out how many kids you'll be watching, what hours you'll be working, and if they'll be picking you up or you're expected to get a ride there.

### What You Do – On the Job

Have the parents show you the doors and windows and how they lock. Have them explain any alarm system. Find out where the first aid supplies and fire extinguisher are stored. Ask if there are any special instructions like nap or bed times, using the TV or radio, whether they can play outside or cook.

Always watch the children so they don't get hurt or make messes. Don't leave them alone in order to do the cleaning.

If you hear suspicious noises, if someone comes to the door requesting to use the phone and won't leave, or if you receive unusual or obscene calls, call the police immediately. Do not go outside to check things out and don't let people into the house.

In case of fire, get the children outside and call the fire department from a neighbor's house.

Play games with the children that they enjoy. They won't have as much fun if you just sit and watch. Get involved with them. Let kids help you with the cleaning. They can pick up toys and books. Most children like washing dishes. Be sure that you take any sharp objects out of the sink first.

When the kids get bored, pull out your fun bag and do some of the activities in it. If they don't want to play with these objects anymore, play follow the leader or Simon Says.

**When Parents Get Back**

Let the parents know what you did, including anything that was unusual. Make sure that the customer provides a ride home after dark, or call your parents for a ride. If the customer appears intoxicated, call your parents to come and get you.

Thank customers for the opportunity to babysit their children and let them know you'd like to do it again. Ask them to be a reference for you in the future.

**How to Make It Safe**

Parents, make sure that you meet the parents your child is babysitting for. Also, only let your kids give their babysitting flyers to families who have children.

*Marketing Plan*

The main methods of marketing will be word of mouth, referrals, and flyers posted in your neighborhood. At the end of each babysitting job, offer business cards that your satisfied clients can share with other parents they know.

Spread the word of your business to school mates, your church congregation, relatives, neighbors, and friends. Keep your business cards and flyers handy at all times to give out when the opportunity presents itself. Don't forget about talking to the parents of your brother's or sister's friends. They may want to hire you when they meet with teachers or need a night out alone and since they already know your family, you are a shoe-in for the job.

Online marketing is good, too. Post to your Facebook and/or Twitter account that you are now the proud owner of your own business. Do let your friends and followers know you are available for babysitting, but never give out the specifics, such as who, when, and where your next job is going to be.

## Finances

Expect parents to give you a tip if they think you have done an exceptional job – and congratulate yourself on exceeding your customers' expectations.

Keep track of your earnings in a spreadsheet or a manual table so you know how much you can earn, and how much you have made. Be sure to include the amount of any tips – these are customers you will want to go out of your way to work for again and again.

Your money will earn interest if you open a savings account at the bank and make regular deposits.

If your parents provided the money for your fun bag or box of supplies, consider paying them back from the proceeds of your business. They are sure to be impressed by your responsibility.

***Jordan's Tip****: Get to know the kids you are babysitting and have fun with them. You need to be in control, but remember that they're young and just want to have a good time. If you do a great job, the kids will be asking their parents to hire you again!*

## Business Plan for a Pet Washing/Grooming Service

### *General Description*

This business is perfect for kids aged: 10 – 17 years old

**Mission Statement**: To provide a service to busy people who don't have time to wash and groom their pets:

**Goals and Objectives**: The goal is to create a business that provides a good source of income during the summer months and weekends throughout the year. The objective is to build a reputation for caring service, attention to detail, and reliability.

**Business Philosophy**: Provide a quality, time-saving service.

**Marketing**: The pet washing and grooming service will be marketed as a way for busy working people to have someone else take care of their pets' needs, saving time.

Competitive strengths are in convenience to the customer and value pricing.

Pricing structure is a set fee for the service, dependent on the number of services desired. Develop a rate structure for varying packages.

**What this business teaches** – Reliability, customer service, caring for animals, and handling money.

### *Operational Plan*

#### Inventory & Supplies: What You'll Need

- Large plastic tub
- Hose with sprayer attachment

- Pet shampoo
- Old towels
- Pet brush
- Scissors
- Dog and cat treats

### What You Do – Preparation

Target neighbors, friends' families, extended family members, church members, and senior citizens. Make up a flyer with your business name and rates. Advertise that you will go to the home to wash and groom cats, dogs, or other small animals.

Put all your supplies in the large tub so they are easily transported.

You may need help to handle larger dogs. Ask a parent or sibling to accompany you and help keep a large animal still while washing and grooming.

### What You Do – On the Job

Ask the customer if the animal has had all its shots before beginning. Ask if the owner prefers you use regular shampoo or one that prevents fleas and ticks.

Work outside, when weather permits. It it's cold, see if you can use the owner's bathtub for bathing inside the house.

Keep the animal calm while you are working. Leave the collar on so you have something to hold onto. Scrub down into the skin with the shampoo.

Be careful not to get soap into the animal's eyes.

Rinse the animal well, getting down to the skin, and towel dry.

Brush the fur; use scissors to carefully cut out any bad matting or weeds stuck in the fur. Be gentle as some animals don't like this or may feel pain when the brush encounters a tangle.

When you are done with the grooming, offer the animal a treat. This way the dog or cat will look forward to your next visit.

**How to Make it Safe**

Never wash and groom an animal that shows signs of illness or bad temper.

Don't offer to clip nails or fur – this could be dangerous if the animal doesn't like it or your hand slips. They could start bleeding.

Parents, help your child as necessary and transport/ accompany them to each job.

## Marketing Plan

The main method of marketing will be flyers and word of mouth to family members, schoolmates, friends, church members, etc. Post your flyer at a veterinary office, the animal shelter, the bulletin board at a senior community (lots of older people have small dogs and cats for companionship), the grocery store, and throughout your neighborhood. Ask permission when posting at a business.

Be sure to take your business cards with you and hand one out to each customer so they can spread the word. Ask customers for referrals.

Take a walk in your neighborhood. Any time you see pets in a yard, leave a flyer on the front door or in the mailbox.

Hold a neighborhood dog wash on a specific weekend. Invite your friends, neighbors, and family members to bring their pets. Ask for a donation for each animal you wash. You can advertise this with a small classified ad in your local newspaper or hold it in conjunction with a neighborhood yard sale.

## Finances

Keep track of your earnings so you know how much you are making, less the cost of shampoo and any other supplies. If you receive a tip, include that amount, too.

Your money will earn interest if you open a savings account at the bank and make regular deposits.

If you like this type of work and want to continue, consider taking classes on professional grooming techniques. This will also teach you how best to handle difficult pets safely.

**Jordan's Tip**: *Cats are really difficult to wash! You might just want to stick to dogs!*

## Chapter Four: Make It Real; Make It Real Simple

*"Getting money is like digging with a needle; spending it is like water soaking into sand."* – Japanese proverb

With a simplified business plan, a marketing strategy, and the specifics of your child's venture in place, it is time to move on to the financial aspects of the business. Yep, it's that dreaded word again: money.

Success depends on using a good business model, making sales, and then taking the profits and investing them wisely. This chapter will go over how to set a budget, determine the cost factor and return on investment (ROI), and talking to your child about banking. These are important topics that will serve your children throughout their lifetimes.

Chances are that your young entrepreneur will have to bankroll their business with your money. Never fear, this shouldn't require a lot of capital. If you stick with the business plans provided here and online at www.cashclubkids.com, there aren't any that should cost more than $50 or so and some that require much less – or nothing at all. You may be able to find many of the necessary supplies in your closets and pantry right now.

The important thing to communicate to your kid is that you are not a never-ending source of funding. After you help your son or daughter get started, they should not only pay you back from the proceeds, they should be able to reinvest some of the funds back into their business so that it grows.

This is why a budget is so important. Many kids see the result of their work efforts in cold, hard cash and immediately want to go out and spend it. Parents, you need to steer them back in the right direction.

Develop a budget together. Start with a list of all costs involved. These would include such things as inventory, supplies, transportation costs, advertising, promotion, and anything else that costs money. Some of these will be one-time costs, such as purchasing a bucket to use for washing cars. Other expenses will recur. If your child decides to hold a chicken enchilada sale, then obviously the goods needed to create the dish are always a recurrent cost.

Total the one-time costs and ask your child to pay that amount back as soon as they have accumulated enough money to do so. After that, they can start fresh with a budget, using their own hard-earned cash.

Make a spreadsheet of all expenses and income. This could be as simple as a handwritten table or one that is put into spreadsheet software, such as Excel, or an accounting program like QuickBooks, and uses automatic calculations. If your child is particularly computer-savvy (and how many aren't these days?), ask your child to develop his or her own budget. This is a great exercise that really puts the financial aspect of their business into perspective.

Perform recordkeeping on a monthly basis, keeping track of all income and expenses with a subtotal by month.

At first it will be difficult to determine actual costs for a venture like a car washing business because one bottle of detergent will last over several jobs. By keeping track of when supplies run out over a period of several months, it will be easier to take that amount and divide it by the amount of sales to come up with an actual cost per job.

Once the real cost is calculated, then your child can figure out how many sales they need to make in order to reach the targeted financial goal. Kids should be encouraged to buy additional supplies and inventory out of the proceeds since this is the way a "real" business works.

If your kid or teen shows a dedicated interest in expanding their business, you can certainly help them do so. You don't want to discourage their entrepreneurial efforts. Perhaps if your son or daughter shows a real affinity for a DJ business, for instance, you could loan them the money to buy more sophisticated equipment. "Loan" is the key word here. Charge interest. There are lots of places online where you can find a simple program to calculate interest charges over a specific period of time; if you have Excel there are several loan calculator templates available for free download.

While we are discussing simple businesses here, do be aware that expansion is always a possibility. There are lots of young entrepreneurs (age nineteen and younger) currently working on their *second million dollars* of income. When it comes to the point that the business moves beyond simple accounting, such as adding capital expenditures and figuring depreciation, then it is a good idea to talk to an accountant or tax professional. The young entrepreneur will need to pay income taxes if the proceeds exceed a certain amount.

After several months of tracking costs and income, your child can create a future forecast. By this time they will know the average cost of sales and how much business to expect and can use those figures to more accurately forecast.

Credit is another consideration. For some businesses, such as music lessons, it may be easier for a customer to pay once monthly rather than at the end of each lesson. This brings up another set of fiscal responsibilities: keeping track of amounts due and preparing invoices. A new spreadsheet works well for this purpose. It need not be any more complicated than a list of customers by name, dates of service, rate for each session, and a place to insert the date of billing and the number of the check received from the customer. Older kids can prepare an invoice. This is a very professional touch which can be easily accomplished using a template in your word processing software.

Ensure that customers know the terms of credit in advance. The easiest way to accept credit for music lessons, for instance, would be to prepare an invoice and present it at the last lesson of the month. Have your child ask for payment right then and there. If he or she runs into a problem with a customer who can't remit immediately or refuses to pay the bill, you may have to step in and see how you might rectify the situation but do give your child a chance to handle it first. If this becomes a common problem, it may be necessary to prepare a written contract ahead of time or stipulate other arrangements for payment.

Previously I mentioned adding in the cost of advertising and promotion to the budget. Use this opportunity to teach any kid, but particularly a teen, how to calculate ROI from various marketing methods. A simple flyer posted in the neighborhood costs very little (the paper and ink) but has the potential of bringing in the majority of customers. That's a really good return.

Take marketing a step further. Help your child place a classified ad in the local newspaper or small community paper like the Thrifty Nickel or Penny Saver. Make sure there is a way to track the responses from the ad included in the text. One simple tracking method is to use a free email account set up just for this purpose. Any inquiries received through this email account will easily show the response rate – without costing a thing. If a phone number is used in the ad, remind your child to ask each caller where they got the information on the business and keep a tally of the responses.

Start a separate spreadsheet for marketing. The total expense of all marketing should be added to the accounting spreadsheet to keep track of costs but it is a good idea to create a separate page to more easily track response rates.

Another aspect of accounting and budgeting involves the opening of a bank account. As we previously discussed, a savings account is probably sufficient for a young child. Older teens should also open a checking account. Not only does this make them feel more mature and responsible, it teaches an additional set of skills always important in life such as writing a check to pay for purchases, balancing a checkbook, and avoiding overdraft fees. Show your child how to keep a running balance, how to transfer money in between a savings and checking account, and how to use online banking, too.

Here's another couple business plans that are perfect for using the good financial practices discussed in this chapter: a jewelry-making business and a personal shopping service.

## Business Plan for
## Jewelry Making & Sales

### *General Description*

This business is perfect for kids aged: 10 – 17 years old

**Mission Statement**: To offer unique, handmade or custom jewelry that is affordable.

**Goals and Objectives**: The goal is to create a part-time business that provides a good source of income by creating jewelry outside of school hours. The objective is to use creativity in making the items for sale, while competing with retail stores for customers.

**Business Philosophy**: Making it easy for kids and adults to buy the jewelry they want to wear.

**Marketing**: Team up with neighbors holding yard sales as a venue for selling your jewelry and/or go door-to-door. Hand out business cards wherever appropriate to find future opportunities.

Competitive strengths are the low prices and convenience of this jewelry "store".

Pricing structure varies according to cost of materials used but should be well below retail store pricing and easily affordable for kids with an allowance.

**What this business teaches** – How to be creative, make change, sales, planning in advance, customer service.

### *Operational Plan*

**Inventory: What You'll Need**

- Jewelry making items (if your town doesn't have a craft store, you can find supplies online)
  - Beads of various shapes, sizes, materials, colors
  - Leather cord in various colors
  - Transparent fishing line
  - Findings (for earrings, necklace clasps, pins, etc.)
  - Fine elastic
- A box with compartments to store your finished pieces
- Money box or envelope
- Coins and bills for change
- Price list
- Order forms (optional)

**What You Do – Preparation**

You will need to create a good inventory of jewelry before you start selling. If you don't have a lot of experience making jewelry, you might want to start with a kit that contains everything you need to learn the basics. Experiment with your creativity. Create pieces that you and your friends would like, but consider making some that adults would wear, too.

Purchase your supplies in bulk to get the best price. Try to buy a lot of different colors and textures of supplies unless you want to specialize in a certain style.

Think about how you are going to price your jewelry. Take into account the cost of supplies along with your time. You may want to visit a retail store and note their prices. The more reasonable your prices are, the more sales you will make to kids who are using their allowance to buy it.

Print up a price sheet. You can post this inside your container or simply print them up on pages that you can hand out to customers.

### What You Do – On the Job

Place your jewelry in the container. Make sure it's easy to see each piece. You may want to line each section of the box with felt so the jewelry stays in place. Use a straight pin to fasten necklaces or earrings to the felt.

Go door-to-door in your neighborhood or set up a table at a yard sale or craft fair. You could also ask stores to take your jewelry on consignment and leave a display on the counter.

Ask your customers if there are any birthdays or special events coming up – they may want to order additional jewelry as gifts. Sometimes asking them reminds them of upcoming events they might have forgotten.

Ask people if they want custom jewelry made (you will want to print an order form if you will be making custom pieces), especially if they don't see anything in your inventory that they like.

Be sure to save money from your sales to repay the upfront costs of the supplies and to replenish them. On a good sales day, you might just sell out!

### How to Make it Safe

Parents, accompany your child if he or she is going door-to-door to sell jewelry.

### Price List

You can copy this list as is or put it into an Excel spreadsheet.

| | Price |
|---|---|
| Bracelet | |
| Ring | |
| Earrings | |
| Necklace | |
| Anklet | |
| Toe Ring | |
| Band | |
| Sets | |
| Cell Phone dangle | |
| Special Order | |

## Special Order Form

| | |
|---|---|
| Name | |
| Address | |
| Phone Number | |
| Description | |
| Price | |
| Deposit Paid | |
| Delivery Date | |

*Marketing Plan*

Create flyers you can post in your neighborhood, at your church, or at school. You might want to include color photos of some of your completed pieces to really show them off. Holidays are a great time to advertise. Prepare a special flyer with a Mother's Day, Valentine's Day, or Christmas theme and hand them out wherever possible, such as at school, in your neighborhood, etc.

Hand out business cards to make people aware of your jewelry sales. Don't forget about neighbors, your siblings' friends, people in your church, and classmates.

Partner with neighbors having yard sales and see if you can set up a table at their sale. Door-to-door sales work well, too. Remember to pass out your business cards and flyers to each customer so they can spread the word.

Host a jewelry party for your friends – either a sleepover or an afternoon tea with drinks and snacks. Let them know in advance you'll be offering your jewelry for sale so they can bring their allowance.

Online marketing is also appropriate. Post to your Facebook and/or Twitter account that you are now the proud owner of your own business. Ask your friends and followers to notify you of any upcoming events where you could set up shop. Take pictures, with permission, of customers wearing your jewelry that you can post to your online photo gallery.

*Finances*

Keep track of inventory cost and your earnings in a spreadsheet or a manual table so you know how much you can earn, and how much you have made. When you review this table later you can easily see which types of jewelry are most popular and profitable – and which are probably not worth your time creating again.

Look for the best deal when buying your supplies. It might be cheaper to order your supplies in bulk online, especially if you don't have a craft store in your town. Dollar stores are good choices, too.

Your money will earn interest if you open a savings account at the bank and make regular deposits.

If your parents provided the money for the cost of your initial inventory, consider paying them back from the proceeds of your business. They are sure to be impressed by your responsibility. Remember to set aside some of your proceeds to pay for more inventory as necessary so you don't have to ask your parents for money again.

***Jordan's Tip****: This is a great business for kids who are creative – and siblings can be a big help.*

*Try putting your pieces together in unique ways, using unusual beads, feathers, crystals, sequins, and things you find around the house.*

## Business Plan for a Personal Shopping Service

*General Description*

This business is perfect for kids aged: 12 – 17 years old

**Mission Statement**: To provide a service to busy people who don't have time to shop for themselves:

**Goals and Objectives**: The goal is to create a business that provides a good source of income during the summer months and weekends throughout the year. The objective is to build a reputation for reliability, shopping savvy, and the ability to stay within a budget.

**Business Philosophy**: Provide a quality time-saving service.

**Marketing**: Personal shopping service will be marketed as a way for busy working people to employ someone else to do the shopping for gifts, groceries, or other items.

Competitive strengths are in convenience to the customer and personalized customer service.

Pricing structure is a set fee for the service, on top of the cost of items being purchased.

**What this business teaches** – Reliability, organization, staying within budget, customer service, handling money, how to compare prices.

*Operational Plan*

**Inventory & Supplies: What You'll Need**
- Transportation

- Phone
- Interview form
- Binder for customer information
- Order form
- Shopping list

**What You Do – Preparation**

Target neighbors, family members, church members, and senior citizens. Make up a flyer with a cute name for your business, such as "Annie the Shopper". List out the types of things you will shop for and advertise your affordable rate for this service.

Your job is to find out what people need and what types of things they want. This starts with an interview, either in person or over the phone. There's a sample interview form at the end of this section you can use for reference.

Keep a binder organized by customer name that contains the interview form with all their personal information and a record of all the orders they've placed. This makes it easier next time you need to go shopping for them again.

Research the cost of the items requested. Look for sales and coupons online and in your local newspaper. Your customer will appreciate your research into finding the best deal.

Obtain the customer's money up front so you don't have to use your parents' money.

Ask your parent to provide transportation. Try to organize your jobs so that you can shop for more than one customer at a time; preferably at a mall or shopping center to limit travel time. Make a list of the items you are shopping for and map out the stores you need to visit. If you find a new store you've never visited before, it's helpful to the parent driving to print out driving directions and a map from MapQuest.

If you will be shopping for a customer who needs something like groceries on a regular basis, be sure to create a calendar to keep track of the days you are scheduled to deliver the order.

### What You Do – On the Job

Shop carefully to stay within budget and satisfy the customer's instructions.

Keep all the receipts in your purse, fanny pack, or a folder to present to the customer, along with their change. You may be asked to return some items, so you will need the receipt for that, too.

If you are unsure about an item you find being what the customer wants, give them a call and ask or buy more than one option to give them a choice.

Don't be afraid to enlist the help of a sales clerk at the store. It will save time if you describe the item you are seeking and ask if the store carries it in stock. If not, they might be able to suggest an alternate store for you to visit.

### Delivery

Perishable items, such as groceries, will need to be delivered to the customer immediately. For other types of items, make an appointment for delivery.

Bring the bags and boxes to your customer at their home or place of business. Show your purchases one by one and make sure they approve. If not, offer to return the items.

Don't have anything gift wrapped until the customer approves the purchase.

Provide receipts and change.

**How to Make it Safe**

Parents, help your child post flyers by placing them around your office or handing out to acquaintances. Accompany your child to in-person interviews. Provide transportation for their shopping trips and deliveries.

**Interview Form**

Name_____

Address_____

Contact
Information_____

Favorite color_____

Colors/Styles in Home_____

_____

Spouse Name/Birthdate/Anniversary_____

_____

Family Members/Birthdates_____

_____

Additional Information_____

_____


**Order Form**

Item_____

Size/Color/Style_____

Description_____

Purpose of purchase (gift, self, etc.)_____

_____

IF GIFT:

Age of recipient_____ Favorite color_____

Gift wrapping?          Yes     No

Boy or girl?_____ Budget (maximum)_____
Money received_____ Date requested_____
Delivery date and time_____

Groceries (write-in list):

_____          _____

_____          _____

_____          _____

_____          _____

_____          _____

_____          _____

_____          _____

_____          _____

*Tip: Keep copies of all lists so you can refer back to them to make future orders easier for your customer.*

*Marketing Plan*

The main method of marketing will be flyers and word of mouth to family members, schoolmates, friends, church members, etc. Post your flyer at the grocery store, the bulletin board at a senior community, the senior citizens center, medical offices, and in neighborhood office buildings. Many older people or those with medical conditions find it difficult to shop for themselves.

Be sure to take your business cards with you and hand one out to each customer when you deliver their order. Ask customers for referrals.

Be friendly and approachable when you are out shopping. Offer assistance to elderly or handicapped shoppers and let them know about your business. If you see someone who is obviously searching for the perfect gift, offer to help them, too, and explain that this is your business.

*Finances*

Keep careful track of the money you receive and how much change is owed back to your customer. It is a good idea to keep a log book and a separate place to store the money (like a money bag or fanny pack) until you have done your shopping. If you receive a tip, indicate that in your log book so you know exactly how much you have earned.

Never, ever, "borrow" any of your customer's money with the intent to pay it back. Wait until you've made a profit before you buy something for yourself.

Your money will earn interest if you open a savings account at the bank and make regular deposits. Some people may want to pay you with a check so a bank account will make it easier to handle this form of payment.

As you get more experienced, consider charging a bit more for your services – especially if you have a particularly picky customer who asks for lots of returns.

*Jordan's Tip: Shopping is fun and you can invite your friends along! If you like going to the mall, why not make money while you're at it?*

## Chapter Five: Practice More Than You Play

*"An ounce of practice is worth more than tons of preaching."* – Mahatma Ghandi

The majority of kids are just like adults when it comes to learning; they retain much more information by doing than just by watching or listening. Before you go out with your child on his or her first job, practice so they feel more comfortable dealing with customers. This is something new to a kid and it can be a bit scary selling their products or services to strangers.

Practicing and rehearsing is something that should involve the whole family. Have your young entrepreneur call a sister or brother on the phone or pretend they are walking up to a neighbor's house and have dad or mom answer it. Not only is this great practice, it's a lot of fun!

Develop a script that your child can read or memorize. I've included some sample scripts in several of the business plans in this book, but you could certainly personalize one that fits in perfectly with your kid's venture. The keys to a good script are: politeness, introduction, sharing the goal and why your child is trying to achieve it, and, of course, the main point of the message, which is to ask for a sale. A good sample script might read something like this:

"Hi, I'm Lauren and I'm offering DJ services for parties. Do you have a minute to speak with me? Great. I'm thirteen years old and I've started my own business to raise money for a summer trip to Washington, DC with my church youth group. I noticed you are hosting a block party next week. Would you be interested in having some music for your event? Since I'm just starting out my rates are very affordable."

Alternately, your child could offer to work for a donation: "The cost is whatever you are willing to pay me!"

This type of script relates all the important information while staying brief and to the point.

Role playing can extend farther than the initial contact with a potential customer. For some businesses, like a DJ, this could make a real difference in the quality of the service and your child's comfort level. The more he or she practices what to do on location, the better the chance of success. And the more successful they become, the more apt they are to stay motivated.

Because customer service is a vital part of any successful business, consider switching roles. Have your young entrepreneur play the part of a customer so they get a better idea of what it is like on the other end of the relationship.

Upon the completion of each role playing exercise, ask your child what he or she learned from the experience. Help her put that knowledge into perspective and use it to be a better businessperson. For example, talk about people who get angry when disturbed for any reason. Figure out an approach that is non-offensive; perhaps appealing to the person's vanity such as, "That's a really great car you've got. I'd like to have a similar one someday. As a matter of fact, that's what I'm earning money for right now. I'd love to be able to wash your car and see it shine."

It is important to set expectations beforehand, too. Be frank with your child and let them know they won't always get a positive reception. They won't make every sale. Sometimes they won't get any sales in a day. Role playing helps with this aspect, too. Have your child rehearse in advance what he will say in response to common objections. Play the part of cantankerous customer and say things like:

- "Your price is too high."
- "I don't have time for this right now."
- "I live alone. I don't have need for (fill in the blank)."
- "Will you guarantee my satisfaction?"
- "I already buy (fill in the blank) at the store."

Communication is a vital skill in any type of business. Too often our educational system fails in this regard. Kids graduate from high school without knowing how to speak in a professional manner or how to write a letter in the proper format using good grammar. These days it's quite acceptable to use slang in speech and emoticons in writing. I don't know about you, but I want my children to learn the proper way to talk and write.

There are many ways to develop effective communication skills in a young person. Some kids are naturally more shy than others so it will take a bit more work to make them comfortable speaking in front of strangers. While it comes naturally to my daughter Jordan, it would really pain my son Ben to initiate a conversation. Remember to work with your child's personality, focus on their strengths, and help overcome their weaknesses in order to make this process less stressful for all. Here are some ideas for teaching your young entrepreneur how to communicate in a professional manner. Have them:

- Join the youth chapter of the Toastmasters International group in your city.
- Call a utility company and ask a question about the bill.
- Write a letter to someone famous whom they admire and ask for a signed photo.
- Research hard-to-find information such as the value of an antique in your home or where to buy an automotive accessory by contacting appropriate vendors.
- Go into a store and ask for directions.

Use the following exercises to mentor your budding entrepreneur and help him or her further develop creative thinking and business skills. These are great for spending quality, one-on-one time as well as promoting an entrepreneurial mindset.

Exercises outside the home:

- Drive around your town and stop at strip malls or shopping centers. Find an empty store and ask your child, "What do you imagine could go in this empty space?"
- Take your son or daughter into your own place of work. Show them how to use the copier or fax machine.
- Visit a retail store and have your child ask for help from a clerk, then purchase an item. Afterward,

have them rate the experience for professionalism, customer service, attention to detail, and satisfaction.

- Attend real estate open houses. Have your son or daughter go through the space as if they were a potential buyer. What are they looking for? What would make them buy? Why would they not consider the purchase?

Exercises to do at home:

- Order some magazines and catalogs or use some you already have. Look through the pages and ask your child which advertisements or products catch their eye and why. Which would they spend their hard-earned money on?
- Go through the newspaper. Review public notices, new business and bankruptcy filings. Talk about the significance of each one and possible causes, such as why an individual might have to declare Chapter 11.
- Play the lottery without purchasing a ticket. Have your child pick a set of numbers and then compare them to the winning numbers. What would he do if he'd won the jackpot?
- Watch a shopping network on television. Pick an item around the house and ask your son or daughter to pitch it to an imaginary audience.
- The invention game: ask your child to come up with their own invention, or an improvement on an existing product or system. Go through the step-by-step process of developing their invention, applying for a patent, and then pitching to a company (either real or imaginary).

- Have your son or daughter pay the family bills for a month. Show them your checkbook balance and ask them to allocate the appropriate amounts for utilities, groceries, and entertainment, etc.

These are just some of the ways you can help develop an entrepreneurial drive and mindset in your child. They are fun games, but they also teach some important skills and lessons while encouraging creativity. If you have several kids aged seven and older, you can do these exercises as a group activity. It can be very enlightening to see how each child acts and thinks differently. With the large size of my family, I've seen this firsthand; all the kids definitely have distinctive personalities and skills.

There are a couple more business plans I'd like to share with you now: one for a lawn care service and one for eBay photography.

## Business Plan for a
## Lawn Care Service

*General Description*

This business is perfect for kids aged: 13 – 17 years old

**Mission Statement**: To provide a service to busy people who don't have time to weed, mow the lawn, and take care of their yard.

**Goals and Objectives**: The goal is to create a business that provides a good source of income during the summer and fall months. The objective is to build a reputation for commitment, attention to detail, and reliability.

**Business Philosophy**: Provide a quality, time-saving service.

**Marketing**: The lawn care business will be marketed as a way for busy working people to have someone else take care of their yard, saving time. It will also be marketed to senior citizens and other people who may have a hard time doing this work themselves.

Competitive strengths are saving the customer time and value pricing.

Pricing structure is a set fee for the service, dependent on the number of services desired. Develop a rate structure for varying packages.

**What this business teaches** – Reliability, customer service, and handling money.

*Operational Plan*

**Inventory & Supplies: What You'll Need**

- Lawn mower
- Weed whacker
- Blower (optional)
- Stepladder
- Extension cord(s)
- Hedge trimmers
- Sprayer bottle
- Weed/insect killer
- Hula hoe (for weeds)
- Set of various sized limb cutters
- Container for your supplies (like a 10 gallon paint can or plastic tub)
- Heavy duty garbage bags
- Bottled water

### What You Do – Preparation

Target neighbors, friends' families, extended family members, church members, and senior citizens. Make up a flyer with your business name and rates. Advertise that you will go to the home to weed, clean up debris, mow the yard, and trim bushes. You can also go door-to-door to find customers.

Put all your smaller supplies in the container so they are easily transported.

Make sure all your equipment is working properly. Gas up the mower and weed whacker, if necessary.

Apply sunscreen and wear appropriate clothing, such as a hat, sturdy shoes, pants, gloves, and eye protection.

Develop several packages with different price levels. One package might be just lawn mowing and weed eating; another might be that plus plant care; a third would add debris removal and tree trimming. Also come up with a price for one-time, weekly, and monthly service.

### What You Do – On the Job

Ask the customer which package they would prefer and quote the appropriate price. Plan on spending at least an hour for lawn mowing and weed eating; longer for bigger packages.

Start early, especially on really warm summer days. Be sure to drink enough water so you don't get dehydrated. Take breaks in the shade as necessary.

If the customer has outdoor pets, ask them to secure the animals before you begin working.

Start with the biggest jobs and areas first. Begin with mowing, then weed eat around the edges of the lawn. From there you can move on to weeding, trimming, and picking up trash. As you go, place the debris in a garbage bag so it's easier to clean up after the job is done. Ask the customer if he or she uses a separate trash bin for yard waste or if they want to start a mulch pile.

When you are done with your work, ask the customer to look over the yard to be sure you didn't miss anything.

### How to Make it Safe

Have mom or dad train you regarding the proper way to use the equipment. It can be dangerous, so take your time and practice good safety habits.

Be on the lookout for ant hills, bee hives, and wasp's nests. Keep away from them; notify the homeowner if you think there is a hazardous situation.

Parents: Make sure your child is wearing the right type of clothing and knows how to safely use each piece of equipment. Go over proper handling and disposal of chemicals.

## Marketing Plan

The main method of marketing will be flyers and word of mouth to family members, schoolmates, friends, church members, etc. Post your flyer at the grocery store, the bulletin board at the senior citizens center, and throughout your neighborhood. Ask permission when posting at a business, such as a hardware store.

Be sure to take your business cards with you and hand one out to each customer so they can spread the word. Ask customers for referrals.

Take a walk in your neighborhood. Any time you see a yard that needs attention, leave a flyer on the front door or in the mailbox. If you see work going on at someone's house, like a swimming pool being built, go up to the door and offer to do the clean up after the job is done.

## Finances

Keep track of your earnings so you know how much you are making, less the cost of gas, equipment, chemicals, and any other supplies. If you receive a tip, include that amount, too.

Your money will earn interest if you open a savings account at the bank and make regular deposits.

If you like this type of work and want to continue, consider investing in commercial equipment that will make jobs easier.

***Jordan's Tip****: Bringing along your iPod so you can listen to music while you work makes the time go faster.*

## Business Plan for Photography for eBay

### General Description

This business is perfect for kids aged: 11 – 17 years old

**Mission Statement**: To provide a service to people who want to sell items online but don't know how to take and upload digital photographs.

**Goals and Objectives**: The goal is to create a business that provides a good source of income during the summer, on weekends, and after school hours. The objective is to build a reputation for great service and increase the customer's chances of getting their items sold.

**Business Philosophy**: Provide a quality service that saves time or bridges the gap between need and skill set.

**Marketing**: The eBay photography business will be marketed as a way for busy working people to have someone else do the time-consuming work of taking photographs of items to sell online. It will also be marketed to senior citizens and other people who might not know how to do this themselves.

Competitive strengths are time savings and convenience.

Pricing structure is a set fee for taking each photograph, editing, and uploading.

**What this business teaches** – Creativity, customer service, computer skills, and handling money.

### Operational Plan

**Inventory & Supplies: What You'll Need**

- Digital camera (good quality) and USB cable
- Computer
- Photobucket account
- Portable light with clip
- Nickel
- Fabric to use as backdrop

**What You Do – Preparation**

Get comfortable with your camera. Go over all the features so you know how to zoom, correct the lighting, save, etc.

Make sure the camera is fully charged and has an empty media card in place.

Practice taking pictures of objects around your house. Find out the best ways to show off certain features, such as using a nickel next to the item to show its size. Experiment with different colors of fabric for the backdrop; dark objects will look better against white or light colors and vice versa.

Spend some time browsing eBay. Note what other people's pictures look like and take tips from successful buyers as to what the photos show in regards to details, marks, etc.

Open an account at Photobucket or a similar photo sharing site. This makes sharing and transferring files easier.

Set up appointments with your customer. Find out their address and ask for a day and time that is convenient for them.

Consider expanding your business to earn more money. You could offer a whole package to customers that consists of taking the photographs, setting up the eBay account, and maintaining the listings. Alternately, you could set up your own eBay store and sell someone else's items on consignment in exchange for a percentage of the purchase price.

### What You Do – On the Job

Ask the customer how many items they have to photograph so you can schedule enough time for each job.

Find an appropriate place to set up the backdrop and the items you are photographing. Against a wall or on a table is usually best. Try to use natural light from windows. If the room is very dark, set up your light in front of or to the side of the item so that it can clearly be seen.

Take as many photos as necessary. Find the best angle(s) to show off the item. Try several different angles and backdrops.

After you are done, review them with the customer and let them pick out the ones they want to use online.

Upload the files directly to the customer's eBay pages, using their computer, or go home and upload them to Photobucket. If the photos need any editing, such as cropping or lightening, you will probably have to do that with your computer. When finished, email the customer the URL to the pictures.

### How to Make it Safe

Don't try to move large objects like a big painting or anything heavy. Leave it where it is and do your best to take a good photo.

Parents, accompany your child to the customer's home or workplace. Never let them enter a stranger's home alone.

## Marketing Plan

The main method of marketing will be online. Post notice of your business on your social media accounts and in forums and group sites. You may want to place advertisements on Craig's List and create a listing for your business in a local online directory such as Yahoo! Local.

If your town has a consignment shop (many antique stores take consignments), ask the owner if you can post a flyer there. Often times if a customer's consignment piece doesn't sell there, they will try to sell it online.

Attend yard sales. Hand your business card to the person holding the sale and offer to post any unsold items on eBay.

You can also use word of mouth and tell family members, schoolmates, friends, church members, etc. about your business.

Be sure to take your business cards with you to each job and hand one out to customers so they can spread the word. Ask customers for referrals, too.

## Finances

Keep track of your earnings so you know how much you are making. You shouldn't need to buy any other supplies after start-up (unless you want to upgrade your camera or computer) so everything you earn is profit.

Your money will earn interest if you open a savings account at the bank and make regular deposits.

***Jordan's Tip***: *If you like this job, you could start another business taking photographs and selling them to websites like stock.xchng.com.*

## Chapter Six: Talking Business

*"Every sale has five basic obstacles: no need, no money, no hurry, no desire, no trust."* – Zig Ziglar

If your kid or teen is going to have a "real" business, you need to teach them the basic tenets behind the offerings of all successful companies. These are: speed, quality, price, convenience, unmet needs, and the "cool factor". Every sale addresses one or more; a product or service must either save time, be of exceptional, lasting quality, be offered at a reasonable price (in direct relation to quality), make someone's life easier, meet a specific need, or simply appeal to a person's desire to look better, feel good, or fit in.

It is important for the young entrepreneur to address these issues in their own business. Experience, research, and knowledge help. Then again, we can use that standard marketing mix of the four Ps – product, price, place, and promotion – to aid the process.

The product of your child's business is either an actual tangible or a service. What they select is based largely on their skill set and their interests. But it also needs to appeal to prospective customers.

A speedy and convenient product is one that saves someone time and trouble. For instance, in the car washing business plan, I've outlined the process as going door-to-door to people's homes and offering the service. Is this speedy? Absolutely. It saves a lot of time for the vehicle owner since the only thing required is paying for the service. Is this convenient? Sure it is. It eliminates the need to drive somewhere else and have it done, or do it themselves.

Quality and the cool factor are also components of the product. Washing a car can certainly be accomplished with varying levels of quality. Some kids – particularly *Executors* – are really great at paying attention to the little details, like shining hub caps and polishing the bugs off bumpers. The higher the quality, the more the service is worth.

What about the cool factor? A clean and shiny car certainly appeals to people who take pride in ownership of their vehicle. When they drive down the street and receive admiring glances, it makes them feel good.

Of course every product has to meet a need. That need may be based on speed, convenience, quality, or the cool factor – or a combination of all these things. Anyone who owns a car has a need to keep it clean. The car washing service addresses that need. However, not every type of venture your child selects is going to fit this requirement. Some kids might prefer to start a business based on their love of playing video games, but it's difficult to imagine turning this into a product that meets anyone's needs but their own! Then again, if they can turn that passion into creating a new video game, it does become a product that meets someone else's need.

The second P is price. In every business plan I've included in this book I advise the young entrepreneur either to take a donation or price their product or service well below retail/ professional levels. Youngsters are not competing with established businesses; they are selling something that allows them to make money to obtain a future goal. They are not operating out of a storefront with associated overhead costs; they are doing this cheaply and passing the savings along to their customers.

Place is the marketing factor that refers to distribution. In the case of the young entrepreneur, this really denotes where and when they sell their product. I always encourage kids to start with the safest, most obvious places to sell such as in the neighborhood, at the homes of friends, to relatives, or church members, or at a public event. I'm sure there are a lot more possibilities but that will depend on your own personal circumstances.

If you run your own retail business, for instance, you might consider showcasing your daughter's handmade jewelry at the cash register. Your son or daughter could also sign up as a vendor at a community craft fair or Christmas bazaar, accompanied by a parent. Church or neighborhood yard sales are another great venue for selling just about anything. Get creative in finding vending opportunities. If your child is the only seller offering a particular product or service at an event, she is bound to be successful simply due to lack of competition.

The final P is promotion, or advertising. The cheapest, and some of the most effective, forms of promotion for the young entrepreneur are posting flyers and word of mouth. Of course, the means of marketing a business are nearly endless, but I'm assuming that most kids and teens won't have a marketing budget in place and will need to rely on inexpensive or no-cost methods of promotion.

This also includes online advertising but I always caution parents to oversee the process. Keep your child safe by limiting the amount of information posted online and available to anyone surfing the 'net. Make sure they never, ever post your home's physical address. I encourage you to set up a free email account to keep things anonymous until an interested party's identity can be verified. I also suggest that you accompany your child on at least the first visit to a customer's home – even if it is someone you know.

If your child bears in mind the various business factors, along with the four Ps of marketing, they are bound to be successful. Use the following two business plans for pool cleaning and newsletter writing businesses to discuss these concepts with your young entrepreneur. Ask him or her to identify the speed, quality, price, convenience, needs, and cool factors of these services and determine if either one is a venture of interest.

## Business Plan for a
## Pool Cleaning/Maintenance Service

### General Description

This business is perfect for kids aged: 13 – 17 years old

**Mission Statement**: To provide a service to busy people who don't have time to take care of their swimming pool.

**Goals and Objectives**: The goal is to create a business that provides a good source of income during the spring, summer, and fall months. The objective is to build a reputation for commitment, attention to detail, and reliability.

**Business Philosophy**: Provide a quality, time-saving service.

**Marketing**: The pool cleaning and maintenance business will be marketed as a way for busy working people to have someone else take care of their swimming pool, saving time and keeping it in good working order.

Competitive strengths are saving the customer time and value pricing.

Pricing structure is a set weekly or monthly fee for the service. Offer a discount for customers who sign up for once a week servicing every month.

**What this business teaches** – Reliability, customer service, and handling money.

### Operational Plan

**Inventory & Supplies: What You'll Need**

- Pool chemicals (you might want to keep some common chemicals like chlorine on hand but it's best to use the customer's products)
- Plastic tote bin
- Net with long handle
- Pool brush with long handle
- Scrub brush
- Tile cleaner (safe for pools)
- Chemical testing kit
- Bottled water

### What You Do – Preparation

Target neighbors, friends' families, extended family members, church members, etc. Make up a flyer with your business name and rates. Advertise that you will go to the home to clean and maintain a swimming pool as a one-time service or on a weekly basis.

You can also go door-to-door to find customers. See if you peek into the backyard to determine if the house has a pool.

Put all your smaller supplies in the container so they are easily transported. If you are using any of your own chemicals, don't close the lid.

Apply sunscreen and wear appropriate clothing, such as a hat, shoes with gripping soles, and eye protection.

Do some comparison shopping to see what other pool services charge. Come up with a price for one-time, weekly, and monthly service. You may also want to perform seasonal maintenance, such as getting the pool ready for winter or doing a deep cleaning before the first summer swim.

## What You Do – On the Job

Ask the customer which package they would prefer and quote the appropriate price. Plan on spending at least an hour for light maintenance; longer for pools that need a deep cleaning and shock treatment. Also ask the customer what type of chlorination system the pool uses and where the chemicals are stored.

Start early, especially on really warm summer days. Be sure to drink enough water so you don't get dehydrated. Take breaks in the shade as necessary.

If the customer has outdoor pets, ask them to secure the animals before you begin working.

Start by testing the water for levels of chlorine, alkalinity and PH. Add the appropriate chemicals to adjust the levels as necessary. Some chemicals are mixed and then dumped into the pool, others have to go in the skimmer basket. Read the labels to make sure you are using the chemicals correctly.

If the pool is green or just dirty, use a shock treatment. Also, if you live in a really hot area, shock treatment should be added about once a week. Remember to tell the customer when you added it so that they don't get into the pool until it is safe (usually twelve hours after shocking). You may have to return the next day to finish cleaning if you have to shock the pool.

If the customer requests you add an algae inhibitor, you can add this to the skimmer.

Empty the skimmer basket of leaves and debris. Use your net to catch any floating debris; empty it right away so it doesn't dry inside the net. Run the pool vacuum to pick up debris along the pool's bottom. You may have to sweep up dirt from the bottom with your long-handled brush so that the vacuum sucks it up.

Check the floating chlorine dispenser (if used) or the filter for chorine sticks and add more, if necessary.

If the decorate tiles along the rim of the pool show signs of algae or mineral deposit, use your tile cleaner and brush to clean them.

Once a month the system needs to be back-flushed. Check the pump equipment for manufacturer's directions on how to do this; it should be posted on the door on a label. Pay close attention to the pressure gauge. While you are there, check the filters for dirt or clogging and clean with a spray of water when necessary.

Pump maintenance should be left to professionals. If you notice any strange noises or obvious signs of a problem, notify the customer.

**How to Make it Safe**

Have mom or dad train you regarding the proper way to use chemicals safely. It can be dangerous, so take your time and practice good safety habits. If you don't have your own swimming pool to practice on and train on proper chemical use, this is probably not a good business for you.

Parents, make sure your child is wearing the right type of clothing and knows how to safely handle chemicals. Encourage them to closely read the labels on all chemicals. You should read them, too, and know what to do in case of accidental splashing in the eyes or on the skin.

*Marketing Plan*

The main method of marketing will be flyers and word of mouth to family members, schoolmates, friends, church members, etc. Post your flyer at the grocery store, and throughout your neighborhood. Ask permission when posting at a business, such as a pool supply or home improvement store.

Be sure to take your business cards with you and hand one out to each customer so they can spread the word. Ask customers for referrals.

Take a walk in your neighborhood. Any time you see a house with a pool, leave a flyer on the front door or in the mailbox, or just go up and knock on the door.

## Finances

Keep track of your earnings so you know how much you are making, less the cost of any equipment and supplies. If you receive a tip, include that amount, too.

Your money will earn interest if you open a savings account at the bank and make regular deposits.

If you like this type of work and want to continue, consider taking a training course in pump maintenance and professional water testing.

*Jordan's Tip: Bringing along your iPod so you can listen to music while you work makes the time go faster.*

## Business Plan for Newsletter Writing

### General Description

This business is perfect for kids aged: 12 – 17 years old

**Mission Statement**: To provide a service to business people and others who want to stay in contact with customers, neighbors, or family members.

**Goals and Objectives**: The goal is to create a business that provides a good source of income during the summer, on weekends, and after school hours. The objective is to build a reputation for excellent writing and design skills.

**Business Philosophy**: Provide a quality service that saves time or bridges the gap between need and skill set.

**Marketing**: The newsletter writing business will be marketed as a way for busy working people to have someone else do the time-consuming work of putting together, writing, and printing a newsletter.

Competitive strengths are quality, time savings, and convenience.

Pricing structure is a set fee for creating each newsletter. Additional fee can be charged if the writer is tasked with providing content.

**What this business teaches** – Creativity, customer service, computer skills, and handling money.

### Operational Plan

**Inventory & Supplies: What You'll Need**

- Computer

- Software, such as Microsoft Publisher
- Color inkjet printer
- Flash drive (optional)
- Clip Art

**What You Do – Preparation**

There are many different types of people you can target: small business owners, neighborhood associations, people with a lot of family members who live far away, even other, young entrepreneurs!

Use a software program you are comfortable with. Microsoft Word and Microsoft Publisher both provide templates for lots of different kinds of newsletter. All you have to do is plug in the information and add/change pictures. Practice making your own newsletter before offering to do it for someone else – plus this will give you an example to show to potential customers.

Think about creating your own themes that can be used for a variety of newsletter types. Combine specific fonts, colors, and design elements that all work well together. It's usually best not to use more than two or three different fonts on one piece.

See if you can find some newsletters online to look at for ideas. Pay attention to how the newsletter author used lines, colors, and graphics to make it interesting.

A lot of people don't know what to put in a newsletter to fill up space. Find some resources with quotes, trivia, statistics, and other little bits of information that you can use in small, blank spots.

If you want to earn more money per job, offer to print mailing labels and mail the newsletter out for the customer (unless they are sending it electronically).

### What You Do – On the Job

Ask the customer about the details of the job: whether or not they've already got content written up, how often the newsletter will go out (how many issues they need you to write), whether or not they have photos to insert, who will be receiving the newsletter, specific colors they want to use, the theme of the newsletter, and how it will be sent (mail or email).

If the customer wants you to write the content, quote a higher price to pay for the time you spend researching and gathering information. When giving a rate for your services, be sure to specify how many revisions the customer can request. This is important because some people are really hard to satisfy and they could ask you to change the newsletter again and again. Allowing for two revisions is good.

If the customer wants you to print the newsletter so they can mail it out, this should be an extra cost since you will have to use ink and paper. Figure out how many pages your printer can produce with one set of color ink cartridges. Take the cost of the cartridges and a ream of paper and divide by the number of copies you can print. That is your per page cost.

Set up a time for a meeting in person.

At the meeting, gather together all the necessary components such as the customer's company logo, their photos, their articles, etc. If you are meeting the customer in their home or place of business, you can use a flash drive to copy all the files, or you can have them emailed to you (sometimes photos are very large files and they can be difficult to email so the flash drive works better).

At home, go to work on creating the newsletter. Start with a template and add articles and graphics where appropriate. Play around with the colors and fonts until you come up with a pleasing design. Don't finish it just yet. Print it out and show the customer or attach the file to an email and ask them for their input. They might want you to change something; it's easier to do that now before you complete the newsletter.

After consulting with the customer regarding their input, go ahead and finish writing the newsletter. Show it to them again and get their approval. Give them printed copies or the file.

**How to Make it Safe**

Parents, accompany your child to the customer's home or workplace. Never let them enter a stranger's home alone.

*Marketing Plan*

Create flyers in color advertising your business. The more professional these look, the better to showcase the quality of your work. You can post them around your neighborhood and at the grocery store but it may be better to have your parents drive you to nearby office complexes and hand them out to each business.

You can market this business online, too. Post notice of your business on your social media accounts and in forums and group sites. You may want to place advertisements on Craig's List and create a listing for your business in a local online directory such as Yahoo! Local. You don't need to stick with local customers, though. If you can correspond via phone or email, you can easily email the file of the completed newsletter to customers located anywhere.

At Christmas time, use word of mouth and tell family members, schoolmates, friends, church members, etc. about your business. A lot of people like to send an annual letter filled with the family's news and updates. This is a great opportunity.

Be sure to take your business cards with you to each job and hand one out to customers so they can spread the word. Ask customers for referrals, too.

## *Finances*

Keep track of your earnings so you know how much you are making, less the cost of supplies (paper, ink, postage, if required). You may want to reinvest some of your profits into new equipment. Keep track of your time, too, so you know how long it takes you to complete a newsletter. Adjust your rate if necessary.

Your money will earn interest if you open a savings account at the bank and make regular deposits.

***Jordan's Tip***: *If you like this job, you could also go into desktop publishing and design advertisements, brochures, and flyers.*

## Chapter Seven: Further Resources

*"The young do not know enough to be prudent, and therefore they attempt the impossible — and achieve it, generation after generation."* – Pearl S. Buck, author

The last thing you want to do is stymie your child's ambition, creativity, motivation, and eagerness. Be sure you have the appropriate resources available to help them get started in entrepreneurship when they are ready. To that end, I've included here some of the best places to find help and accomplish the exercises noted throughout the book.

### *General Resources*

- Cash Club for Kids: Monthly membership site full of business plans, ideas, and products that help your child get started with his or her own business. Monthly contests in several categories for the best young entrepreneurs. Annual camps for the whole family and dedicated conference call support. www.cashclubkids.com
- SCORE: Staffed by volunteers, SCORE offers free business advice for small business start-ups. They have a special section just for young entrepreneurs at www.score.org/young.html

- Junior Achievement: One of the oldest organizations that exists to help young adults achieve entrepreneurial and educational goals. www.studentcenter.ja.org
- Kidzworld: What's Your Job Personality? Free online test to match a child's personality with job skills. http://www.kidzworld.com/quiz/2815-quiz-whats-your-job-personality
- Small Business Administration: Teen Business Link. Business ideas, money management, legal matters. http://www.sba.gov/teens/
- Network for Teaching Entrepreneurship: This organization provides free business training to entrepreneurs aged 11 to 17 in low income areas. http://www.nfte.com/default.asp
- Future Business Leaders of America: Nationwide education association with local chapters for students from middle school on up to college age. Activities, competitive events, conferences. http://www.fbla-pbl.org/
- United States Department of Labor: Office of Disability Employment Policy. Offers education assistance for disabled youth to start their own business. http://www.dol.gov/odep/pubs/fact/entrepreneurship.htm

## Financial/Budgeting

- Microsoft Office: Monthly Income and Expense Tracker for Excel. http://office.microsoft.com/en-us/templates/monthly-and-annual-income-and-expenses-planner-tracker-TC030001675.aspx
- Microsoft Office: Loan Calculator. http://office.microsoft. com/en-us/templates/results. aspx?qu=loan+interest#ai:TC030004740|

- Microsoft Office: Invoice Templates. http://office.microsoft.com/en-us/templates/results.aspx?qu=invoice

*Grants/Scholarships/Competitions*

- Canada One: Grant and loan resources for young entrepreneurs located in Canada. http://www.canadaone.com/magazine/loan_programs.html
- Global Student Entrepreneur Awards: Existing for-profit businesses owned by teens in high school or young adults in college are judged. Finalists share prizes worth $150,000 while the winner is awarded $10,000. http://www.gsea.org/Pages/Default.aspx
- Independent Means, Inc.: Provides scholarships for annual start-up business camp. Annual competition with award of $1,000 to the winner. http://www.independentmeans.com/imi/index.php
- Local: Check into programs available through your city's Chamber of Commerce, major corporations, and school system. Most cities have local programs in place to educate, provide internships, and fund youth start-ups.
- New Mexico Youth Entrepreneurship Network: Annual statewide business plan competition for youth who live in New Mexico; awards up to $800. http://www.nm-youth-entrepreneurs.com/BizPlanCompetition/tabid/419/Default.aspx
- NFIB Young Entrepreneur Foundation: Promotes entrepreneurship through scholarship programs, classroom games and teacher and student programs. http://www.nfib.com/YEF Blog: http://youngentrepreneurfoundation.wordpress.com/

*Resources for Exercises*

- United States Patent and Trademark Office:
  http://www.uspto.gov/
- United States Courts/Bankruptcies:
  http://www.uscourts.gov/FederalCourts/Bankruptcy.asp
  x
- Home Shopping Network online:
  http://www.hsn.com/watch-hsn-
  live_xh.aspx?cm_re=LeftNav*watch*HSNtvLive
- Microsoft Office: Checkbook register.
  http://office.microsoft.com/en-
  us/templates/results.aspx?qu=checkbook+register

Are you ready to help your kids get started with their very own business? I hope you've found the information in this book useful and I wish you the greatest success in raising a responsible young entrepreneur. As a last way to say thank you for buying this book, I am providing a final business plan for a window washing service. Enjoy!

## Business Plan for a Window Washing Service

### *General Description*

This business is perfect for kids aged: 8 – 17 years old

**Mission Statement**: To provide a service to busy people or business owner who don't have time to wash windows.

**Goals and Objectives**: The goal is to create a business that provides a good source of income during the summer and on weekends. The objective is to build a reputation for value, attention to detail, and reliability.

**Business Philosophy**: Provide a quality, time-saving service.

**Marketing**: The window washing business will be marketed as a way for busy working people to have someone else take care of their windows, both inside and out. It will also be marketed to business owners who may need this service at their office.

Competitive strengths are saving the customer time and value pricing.

Pricing structure is a set fee for the service, dependent on the number of windows that need to be cleaned. Develop a rate structure for varying packages such as weekly, monthly, or one time.

**What this business teaches** – Reliability, customer service, and handling money.

### *Operational Plan*

**Inventory & Supplies: What You'll Need**

- Two pails
- Squeegee with telescoping handle
- Stepladder
- Garden hose with spray attachment
- Glass cleaner (you can make your own)
- Cornstarch
- Measuring cup (half cup)
- Coffee filters
- Newspapers
- Soft cotton rags or chamois cloth

**Recipe #1 for Homemade Window Cleaning Solution**
- Plain white vinegar
- Rubbing alcohol
- Half a lemon or bottled lemon juice
- Dishwashing liquid

Take an empty, clean spray container and fill it ¾ full with vinegar. Add rubbing alcohol until the container is almost full. Add juice of half lemon squeezed or about 1 tablespoon of bottled lemon juice. Finish off with a squirt of dishwashing liquid.

**Recipe #2 for Homemade Window Cleaning Solution**
- Pail of warm water
- ½ cup of cornstarch

Mix the cornstarch into the pail of water. Wipe on with a clean cloth and wipe off with wadded up newspaper pages.

**What You Do – Preparation**

Target neighbors, friends' families, extended family members, church members, senior citizens, and small business owners. Make up a flyer with your business name and rates. Advertise that you will go to the home to wash windows both inside and out. You can also go door-to-door to find customers.

Place your supplies in the pails so they are easily transported.

You can buy your cleaning products or make your own. If you are using the cornstarch recipe, bring along a box of cornstarch and a measuring cup so you can mix it up on the spot.

Do some research on the rates that professional window cleaners charge for their service. You rate should be about half. Come up with a price for one-time, weekly, and monthly service – it's easier to keep windows clean if you do it on a regular basis.

**What You Do – On the Job**

Ask the customer how often they would like their windows cleaned and quote the appropriate price. Businesses will probably want you to do the job weekly, especially if they have glass doors that get lots of fingerprints on them.

Start with the outside of the windows. You can use one of those cleaners with a bottle that attaches to the hose to make this easier – especially if you are short and it's hard to reach the top of the window. If not, spray your homemade or commercial cleaner on the outside glass. Use the squeegee to scrape it off and finish by polishing with your clean rag or chamois cloth. Use the stepladder if you need it.

Next, move inside. If you are working in an office, be careful not to disturb employees or customers.

The best way to clean interior glass is to mix up the cornstarch and water recipe and wipe it on the glass with one cloth. Take a clean cloth and dry it off. You can also use wadded up newspaper or coffee filters for the final wipe. Experiment with what works best depending on the time of dirt you encounter. The cornstarch formula works great for streaky glass but you might need the stronger vinegar recipe for getting rid of greasy dirt.

When you are finished, pack your supplies back into the pails and throw away your trash.

**How to Make it Safe**

Parents: Hold the stepladder steady for your child when using. Don't let him or her enter a stranger's home alone. Be sure the child knows how to handle cleaning chemicals safely.

*Marketing Plan*

The main method of marketing will be flyers and word of mouth to family members, schoolmates, friends, church members, etc. Post your flyer at the grocery store, the bulletin board at the local senior citizens center, and throughout your neighborhood.

Go to the office complexes near your house. Drop off a flyer at each business.

Be sure to take your business cards with you and hand one out to each customer so they can spread the word. Ask customers for referrals.

Go door-to-door in your neighborhood and offer your services.

## Finances

Keep track of your earnings so you know how much you are making, less the cost of supplies. If you receive a tip, include that amount, too.

Your money will earn interest if you open a savings account at the bank and make regular deposits.

If you like this type of work and want to expand, consider offering house cleaning services in addition to window washing.

***Jordan's Tip****: Wipe outside windows up and down and inside windows back and forth. That way you can see which side is streaky and needs more cleaning.*